A great read! My friend, Scott, combines his amazing experiences as a sports media professional with personal family experiences and creates an intriguing perspective on the human traits of our sports heroes. This book not only brings back fond memories of my father and playing hockey in Canada, but reminds me of what makes you successful in business and life!

—Bob Schlegel, Chairman and CEO Pavestone Company, L.P.
Chairman of Schlegel Sports Group

Scott steps into the minds of greatness—talented, courageous sports icons who have been a beacon, a source of hope . . . men who merged their God-given gifts with dignity and honor. Walk away from the television and into the pages of *Whatever It Takes*, and revisit life's precious commodities: character, love, and family relationships.

—Janine Turner, Actress

Scott Murray's book portrays the deep love and bond that developed between him and his father through their mutual passion and enjoyment for sports. More importantly, it describes the life lessons imparted from father to son through the study of their sports heroes, attributes that enabled those athletes to be so successful in their fields of endeavor. For fathers raising their children, this book is a terrific read.

—Bobby Brown, MD, Cardiologist; NY Yankees Infielder (1946–54);
American Baseball League President (1984–94)

Scott Murray has rubbed shoulders with some of the greatest names in sports. His book combines the wit, wisdom, and winning attitude he's witnessed on the playing field with what he learned from his mentor, his father. *Whatever It Takes* is a grand slam.

—Ron Kirk, Attorney and Former Mayor of the City of Dallas

WHATEVER
IT
TAKES

WHATEVER IT TAKES

Life Lessons Learned through Sports Legends

Manufactured in the United States of America.

For information, please contact:
Brown Books Publishing Group
16200 North Dallas Parkway, Suite 170
Dallas, Texas 75248
www.brownbooks.com
972-381-0009
A New Era in Publishing™

ISBN-13: 978-1-933285-67-2
ISBN-10: 1-933285-67-2
LCCN 2006933116
1 2 3 4 5 6 7 8 9 10

Cover photo by Richard K. Dalton.
Additional photos courtesy of Brad Bradley.

WHATEVER IT TAKES

Life Lessons Learned through Sports Legends

SCOTT MURRAY

DEDICATION

To my dad, who taught me how to be
a dad to Doug and Stephanie, with all
my respect, love, and admiration.

CONTENTS

FOREWORD

Y ou need to write a book." That's what many kept telling Scott Murray, and now I am happy to report that he finally listened. I knew that he had winning stories to share with adults and children alike about his relationship with a great man who shaped his life and taught him the qualities necessary to strive for excellence—his father. Scott probably didn't know he was creating a story of the very foundation of fatherhood: integrity, leadership, and compassion. From a childhood filled with sports to a career covering that scene, Scott embodies the kind of man whom any parent would be proud to say, "Yes, that's my son."

What I hoped for, but did not expect, is that Scott would be able to share so much of himself in this book. The names of the athletes represented speak for themselves, of course. But Scott's perspective provides a reporter's look at each of these athletes that affords insight into not only their characters but his as well. And as we get to know the latter, we quickly learn that Scott embodies the kind of enlightenment that comes only from the guidance of a loving father.

Reading this book filled with Scott's choices of those people who embody the same qualities of passion, principle, and purpose as his father is not only rewarding but informative and fun. Scott's enthusiasm and perseverance leap from the pages like an inspired, fourth-quarter, ninety-nine-yard kickoff return. His book helps remind us why some athletes truly deserve to be considered heroes and what attributes made them so. I have never had a chance to meet Scott's father, but it's obvious from these pages that Scott considers him a special hero, and he is obviously his biggest fan.

Scott has been a longtime friend. The qualities he inherited from his father are evident in his professional career as an award-winning reporter and commentator. He carries those qualities into his personal life with his involvement in countless civic and charitable organizations that serve many, particularly children.

I'm so happy Scott Murray stepped up to write this book. The next time you see him, let him know we're all waiting for his next effort.

Scott, thanks for sharing your treasured times with your Dad.

Lamar Hunt

Lamar Hunt's numerous accomplishments make him one of the most influential men in the history of sports. His impressive resume includes the following achievements: Founder of both the American Football League and the Kansas City Chiefs; member of eight different Halls of Fame, including the Pro Football Hall of Fame and the Texas Business Hall of Fame; founding investor of the Chicago Bulls; involvement in the development of World Championship Tennis and the North American Soccer League. He presently operates three Major League Soccer franchises.

ACKNOWLEDGMENTS

W hat a thrill it has been recalling the moments, the mentors, and the memories that helped shape the journey I have been privileged to travel. And yet, like almost everything along the way that I was challenged by and learned from, none of it would have been possible without the guidance and support of many. And so, I offer thanks and extend my deepest gratitude to those who were alongside me to share the ride, helping to direct me, counsel me, and inspire me in getting from where I was to where I wanted to be.

People like Dorothy Jo Watts and John Gordon, who believed in me and gave me my first job in radio when I was just a teenager. Or Jack Palvino, whom I woke up to every morning as a kid getting ready for school, and who years later gave me my first full-time job in radio when I was in college. There was crusty ol' George Geib, the general manager of the radio station who told me I needed to be in television or "go back to college and become a doctor like [I] planned to do in the first place." I'll never forget Mike Corken, the first television general manager I ever worked for. He asked me if I could grow a mustache to put a little maturity on my face so I didn't look like his baby-faced paperboy. But Mike and news director Jim Valentine gave me a chance, and that's all anyone can ever ask for. I'll forever be indebted to them for giving me that first opportunity in television news/sports.

My thanks to David Nuell and Jim Van Messel, the pair who brought me to NBC in Washington, D.C. When I eventually left and moved to Dallas–Fort Worth, David and Jim departed D.C. not long after, heading west to Hollywood to become executive producers of a new show called *Entertainment Tonight*, although I'm sure it had nothing to do with my departure.

Bill Vance was the news director who hired me in Texas. I asked management if I could do a Sunday night sports recap show like I had done in Washington. I was told that might be a problem, as the station was airing reruns of *Perry Mason,* and that show was number one in the ratings. Go figure. After some persuading, the station committed to *Scott Murray's Sports Extra,* the first expanded Sunday-night program of its kind in the Southwest. Now there are six such Sunday-night, local-sports recap shows in DFW. Times change.

Special thanks goes to Frank O'Neill, who was my general manager in Texas longer than any other general manager. He was not only my boss but became someone I learned from and respected, and I cherish his friendship—I've stayed in touch with him to this day. It was Frank who convinced me that I should share my experiences and write a book.

I can't begin to thank those who traveled much the same road as I, from directors Jim Borden and Larry Huante, floor director Nate Tarpley, and jack-of-all-trades Terry Briggs, who were all there from day one, to all of the talented sports reporters who joined us along the way, to the hundreds of college interns who learned the practical side of the business with us, students like Sean Hamilton, who would return after graduation and become an award-winning sports producer. And most of the pictures and interviews we shared with our millions of television viewers were courtesy of two of the best in the sports video business, Kerry Smith and Larry Herrera. And certainly, thanks to my news anchor desk mates, Alyce Caron, Brad Wright, Jane McGarry, and Mike Snyder. From reporters to editors, producers to photographers, production assistants to grips, thanks simply doesn't do justice to the people that made up the great teams I had the chance to be a part of over the years.

My thanks to Mike Towle, whose incredible talent, compassion, and heart allowed me to share my thoughts as eloquently, expressively, and effectively as possible. My sincere gratitude to Mike for his far-reaching knowledge, literary wisdom, and cherished friendship. You're a real pro, Mike.

Thanks also to the wonderful publishing team at Brown Books. They never stopped making it fun. From Milli and Kat to the rest of the creative team: Lauren Castelli, Katie Buxton, Allison McCutcheon, Cindy Birne, Ted Ruybal, Brian McKay, and Chad Snyder. You were awesome. I also extend my utmost thanks to my longtime friend Brad Bradley for his generous contribution to my photo gallery.

And even though there are others from the sports world who don't prominently appear in this book, please know that their friendship and the respect and admiration I have for them all is no less important than those who do appear. I'll always cherish the early days and benevolent ways of friends like Don and Linda Carter, who brought NBA basketball to Texas, then handed the torch to Ross Perot Jr. and Mark Cuban as the team matured to the next level. Special Mavericks players, past and present, who have always exemplified character and commitment both on the court and off also deserve mention: Brad Davis, Rolando Blackman, Derek Harper, Michael Finley, Steve Nash and Dirk Nowitzki. Much the same with the Sidekicks' Billy Phillips, Curtis Partain, and Tatu,—the soccer player extraordinaire with an even bigger heart. Norm Green introduced a whole new generation in Texas to NHL hockey, while Tom Hicks allowed the Stars to bring home the state's first-ever Stanley Cup. And Mike Modano, who skates with the grace of a prima ballerina yet the speed of an accelerating Ferrari, helped Texans, as much as anyone, come to appreciate the great sport of hockey just as much as fans have come to embrace his all-star talent and charitable spirit. There was Johnny Oates, the first manager ever to take the Rangers to post-season play, always compassionate and busy with commitments, but always able to make time for you. And baseball's good guys, like Jim Sundberg, Pete O'Brien, Toby Harrah, Mark McLemore, and Steve Buechele, who set the standard for present-day good guys and all-star players, like Derek Jeter and Michael Young. And so many former football players remain fixtures and friends in the Texas community, continuing to make a difference. The list of Cowboys and other gridiron greats is almost endless: Bob Lilly, Tony Dorsett, Drew Pearson, Mel Renfro, Cliff Harris, Charlie Waters, Randy White, Chad Hennings, Bill Bates, Mike Renfro, Tony Hill, Jim Jeffcoat, Darren Woodson, Jay Novacek, Kevin Gogan, Mark Stepnoski, Robert Newhouse, Billy Joe Dupree, Walt Garrison, Lee Roy Jordan, Jethro Pugh, John Fitzgerald, Bob Breunig, Rayfield Wright, Doug Donley, John Dutton, Jason Garrett, John Gesek, Kurt Petersen, Tony Casillas, Russell Maryland, Dat Nguyen, Preston Pearson, Too Tall Jones, Everson Walls, Donnie Anderson, Terry Bradshaw, Billy Sims, and Earl Campbell. From Michael Johnson to Carly Patterson, D.A. Weibring to Bruce Lietzke, Lanny Wadkins to Lee Trevino, Ben Crenshaw to Justin Leonard, they've all thrilled us with their athletic feats while remaining stellar citizens in our community. And I would be remiss if I didn't make note of the people in management who have made a lasting impression over the last quarter of a century, and who also remain good friends. Folks like Don and Donnie Nelson, Rick Sund, Kevin Sullivan, Terdema Ussery, Jim Lites, Bob Gainey, Ken Hitchcock, Jeff Cogan, Gordon Jago, Eddie Gossage, Tom Grieve, Mike Stone, John Blake, Bobby Bragan, Greg Aiello, Rich Dalrymple, Stephen Jones, Jim Meyers, Norv Turner, Joe Avezzano, Gil Brandt, Tom Starr, Rick Baker, and one of the finest men I have ever met, Lamar Hunt—a true sports icon.

Still others outside the sports arena I thank for their wisdom, their counsel, and their friendship: Alan White, Mick Ashworth, Jim Keyes, Bob Schlegel, Bill Lively, Andy Broadus, Barry Andrews, Mike Bourland, Jim Turner, Dr. Bobby Brown, Dr. Bob Cluck, Norman Brinker, Ross Perot Jr., Roy Newman, Bill McLaren, Jay Travers, Chuck Norris, Senator Kay Bailey Hutchison, Richard Greene, Bob Bolen, Ron Kirk, Mike Moncrief, Tom Vandergriff, Congresswoman Kay Granger, Billy Rosenthal, Howard Katz, Norm Miller, Dr. Kenneth Cooper, Marty Leonard, Dr. Gerald Turner, Curtis Hamilton, Bob Lansford, Randall Goss, Dr. Tom Rogers, Wayne Sanders, Charles Ringler, Scott Ginsberg, Bobby Rodriguez, David

Martineau, Ron Haddock, Fin Ewing, John Scovell, Joe Haggar, Boone Pickens, Rod Rohrich, Talmage Boston, Baron Cass, Larry Wansley, Bobby McGee, Ken Schnitzer, Janine Turner, David Holben, Jerry Freeman, Stubbs Davis, and Greg Sampson.

Most of all, I thank my family. My son, Doug, and my daughter, Stephanie are my two greatest gifts. A father could not be prouder of anything or anyone on the face of this earth. And to Carole, who, despite all of her duties as a mom and a best friend, always found time to support my endeavors, even though it often meant taking a back seat so that I might live out my dream. Thank you!

Lastly, I thank my parents. Mom and Dad gave me the greatest gift a parent can give a child. For as far back as I can remember, they both loved me, encouraged me, and dearly believed in me, allowing me to believe in myself.

There is no question that when the final buzzer is sounded, what I'll remember most won't be the homer that won the game or the touchdown that captured the ring; it'll be the individuals that I met, the relationships that were forged, and the memories forever shared.

INTRODUCTION

My memories of my dad date back more than fifty years, and they are as vivid now as they were when I lived them. It's not just the sights; it's also the sounds and even the scents, whether it be the smoke from his pipe or the autumn pleasure of catching the whiff of burning leaves wafting through the neighborhood.

It's he and I playing catch in the backyard of our home just outside Rochester, New York; ours was the house on the corner lot with the yard shaped like an isosceles triangle.

It's throwing the football around on one of those leafy October days, long after an Indian summer has given way to the chill of autumn, the season's first snowfall only weeks away. I go back to a time when a dad and son could share intimate sports moments someplace other than in a noise-filled sports bar or plopped down in front of the satellite-fed TV, watching endless hours of sports. These are year-round memories that include the spoken word between parent and child.

There was also hockey, which is no stranger to upstate New York, where the winters can be gloriously or brutally cold and snowy, depending on how you look at it. There's my dad and me, bundled against the elements, ski tuques on our heads and parkas zippered as high as they go, our mittens clutching hockey sticks as we take turns wristing shots on goal at one another, using the imaginary goal that backs up against the garage.

Our faces are practically frozen, and we can see our breath emanating from our mouths and noses. We speak few words, letting the puck and our hockey sticks scraping along the pavement do most of the talking in between the occasional grunt or burst of laughter as we go at it—Rocket Richard and Jacques Plante doing their thing.

My dad, Douglas, is eighty-three now. If he still had the ability to communicate with me with any level of reasonable cognition—he's been battling prostate and colon cancer and suffering from a form of dementia—he no doubt would chuckle at my sentimentality. I also know, though, that he would be here with me, sharing in the joy of how our shared love of sports over and over again provided a common language through which we could relate to one another.

Dad can't really carry on an in-depth conversation anymore. There is no calling him on the phone during sporting events, like this year's NBA Finals, to compare notes at intermission and talk second-half strategy. Dallas was there for the first time in team history, but there was no sharing the moment with Dad. Those days, sadly, will never return. I also know too well the day will someday come that he won't be here at all, much like the day breast cancer finally got the better of my little sister, Debby. It took her away—one of those family tragedies that begs for a strong countenance to be worn in public, although deep down the edges of one's soul are seared, leaving a heart a bit more hardened than it was months earlier.

I can still hug Dad those times that I visit him, but it's that hug back that I cherish more than anything. I'm already starting to miss him, but I do it knowing that together we have lived a rich life of shared experiences and a love and respect that has been unmatched.

Let me tell you about my dad. He is from Nova Scotia and grew up just outside Toronto, where he came to become an avid Montreal Canadiens fan. (The Maple Leafs never had a chance with him because those early years in Nova Scotia had already forever bonded him with Les Habs.) By the time I was born, my dad and mom had moved to the Rochester area, eventually moving out to a suburb, I guess you could call it, a small town on the Erie Canal named Spencerport.

It was a little bit like Mayberry with snow but not the drawl, and family life resembled an episode of *Leave It to Beaver*. Growing up in the '50s and '60s, I can say that we lived in a terrific neighborhood. The kids played together, the adults interacted with one another, and there was no need to lock up the houses. My parents were also smart enough to put up a basketball goal right outside the house and encourage me to bring kids over to play; that way, they could always keep an eye on me, beckoning my friends and me with treats and snacks so we would keep coming back.

We were the basic middle-class family, and I had the luxury of growing up in a fully functional household. Dad was a project engineer—there's a lot of that around Rochester, which long served or presently serves as the corporate headquarters for such scientific companies as Xerox, Eastman Kodak, Taylor Instruments, Sybron, and Bausch and Lomb—but by no means were we rich. Dad provided for us well, but we never splurged for things like big-ticket items or fancy, two-week vacations touring Europe. When we went on vacation, we didn't fly. It was like the movie *Vacation;* we drove everywhere in the family truckster, although Aunt Edna was never a part of the journey. While they couldn't give expensive gifts, my parents showered us with attention and encouragement. I can't count the number of times my dad had his arm around me or I saw him with his arm around Mom.

Dad rarely yelled at any of us, but he was firm in his admonishments as well as his convictions. Whenever I see a film with Gregory Peck in it, I am reminded of Dad—a man who commands respect without ever demanding it and a strong presence without a shred of intimidation.

He was really good with his hands. I still have in my study these big speakers—beautiful, huge, black walnut cabinet speakers—that he made Carole and me for a wedding present. He had a woodworking shop in our garage, which is why we never parked the car in there when I was a kid. As cold and snowy as it could get, the car still remained outside.

Dad would make anything that we needed for the house. He could fix stuff too. It didn't matter if it involved plumbing or electrical expertise; he knew how to work with it. Handy guy to have around. To this day, three-quarters of the furniture in my parents' house are things that he built. Tables. Hutches. Sound systems. You name it.

As busy as he was at work (and sometimes that would take him away from home for days at a time) and in his woodshop, my dad still was able to make a lot of time for me. He's one of the most balanced people I've ever met, and he believed in black and white when it came to distinguishing right from wrong. There was no gray. He directed and disciplined, but he was never a dictator.

Both of my parents taught through what I call "affection and direction." All those times my dad had an arm around my shoulder, he was constantly suggesting, teaching, planting little ideas in my head, planting the seeds for when the time came in my life that I would be making my own decisions and needing to know right from wrong. One of his philosophies was "nobody's perfect," so when you make a mistake, be accountable, deal with it, and always learn from it.

Most guys with dads like mine will talk about the movie *Field of Dreams,* in which Kevin Costner's character finally gets to have a catch with his father. I loved it too. But the movie that really hits home with me now is *The Notebook.* Unfortunately, that's a slice of Dad's life, as I see it today. Emotional stuff, yet certainly a message about life. I love real-life, feel-good stories that have a message you can learn from. I still get choked up when I see *The Pride of the Yankees,* with Gary Cooper portraying Lou Gehrig.

Dad was all about life's lessons and passed them along to me every chance he got. He was big on being passionate, being productive, and having perseverance. He was big on conviction and courage and character. He was always talking about my having balance in my life, as well as credibility and continuity. He told me these things because they all had been so important in his life.

We did all the things that a father and son should do, and much of what we said to and did with each other centered around sports. It was a language that we shared, a way of being intimate about things without ever really expressing it in those terms. Precious were the days that Dad would sit down next to me with the newspaper and open it to the sports section. We would talk about stuff, and he loved using sports heroes as role models to make a point to me about all those qualities that he espoused as values and virtues.

Like any kid I knew growing up, I collected baseball cards. Shoe boxes were filled with them. My mom is one of the few moms in America who didn't throw all mine out. I've still got them. Over time I got Mickey Mantle to sign six of my cards, one of which I carried around in my wallet for over twenty-five years.

You've heard about Bob Costas carrying that Mantle card around with him all these years? I know well where he was coming from. We both got a big kick out of it the first time we met and compared our wares. Cool stuff. Part of the kid never gets any older.

The Mick is gone now, and someday my father will be as well. There is so much that he did for me through the years, and it goes back as far as I can remember. The backyard catches. Throwing the pigskin around. Trading slap shots in the driveway (sometimes with Mom too). Dad wasn't an emotional person in the sense that he got emotional often or was free in showing his tears. He wasn't that way at all, but he loved me dearly, and he showed it all the time. The hugs. The dinnertime conversations. Those hundreds of hours in the backyard. His teaching me about sports and sportsmanship while we watched *Hockey Night in Canada* together on the old black and white, or sitting me down to tell me about the humility and honor of Lou Gehrig, or the courage and fortitude of Jesse Owens. Those were two of my dad's favorite sports heroes, and through him they became two of mine as well.

One of them I would get to meet; the other was gone before I was ever born. But they both had a lasting impression on me.

The best part about all this for Dad and me is that our lives came full circle. It was through my work in sports television that I was able to repay his gift to me by introducing him to the world of big-time sports and many of the figures he had used as examples while I was growing up.

It was in the mid-1970s, when I was working for a station in Albany, New York, that I got my first chance to give Dad his sports thrill of a lifetime (although there would be more down the road). The Montreal Canadiens and Boston Bruins were playing the Stanley Cup Finals, which, as it turned out, Montreal was in the process of sweeping in four straight games. Games three and four were at Boston Garden, giving me an idea that would involve getting Dad to the Garden.

Carole and I invited my folks over to Albany, and when they got there, Dad and I hopped into my car and drove the two and a half hours to Boston. I had a couple of media credentials, as well as a friend at Boston Garden who was able to get Dad a seat down in one of the corners, right behind the glass, where photographers were positioned to take photos through holes in the glass designed specifically for them. Dad was situated right next to a *Sports Illustrated* photographer.

Between each of the periods I came down from the press box to check on Dad, and while he didn't say much, I could see that he was as giddy as a schoolboy. After the game was over and the Canadiens had wrapped up the Stanley Cup (much to Dad's delight), he got to go out on the ice along with dozens of photographers during the awards ceremony. Camera in hand, he took a lot of pictures in a drawn-out moment that must have felt like a slice of heaven to him.

The best part came when Montreal's Yvan Cournoyer skated around the rink, carrying the Stanley Cup trophy as my dad and others snapped away. Back in Toronto, while all this was unfolding, my uncle Howie, Dad's younger brother, was watching the post-game ceremonies live on TV. Sitting in his den, Uncle Howie leaned closer to the screen where he saw this guy with an uncanny resemblance to his brother, Douglas. In fact, it wasn't just a resemblance; it was his big brother, and for a moment my uncle started wondering if he had lost his mind. He called my mom in Albany and asked her what was going on, if that really was Dougie out on the ice at Boston Garden. Howard had no idea that my dad was going to the hockey game, and he about fell out of his lazy chair when he saw that.

That game at Boston Garden was a huge payoff for my dad. It was everything he could have dreamed of, living the life of a common man outside Rochester, New York, telling his son all these wonderful stories of sports lore. Now, twenty years later, his son was on the other end, giving him the kind of payback that I know not many sons have ever been in a position to give their dads.

There were other moments like this as well, such as when my dad met honorary captains Joe DiMaggio and Willie Mays at baseball's annual All-Star Game in 1977 at Yankee Stadium and then chatted with Steve Garvey, Tom Seaver, and Johnny Bench during batting practice; or the time I took my folks to Cooperstown for the Baseball Hall of Fame induction ceremonies; or when they joined me at Walt Disney World and spent the week with Herschel Walker and Tony Dorsett at the Goofy Games for charity; we also visited nearby Miami so they could enjoy the hoopla of Super Bowl week and all that goes with it, as they prepared to attend the big game on Sunday. Maybe it was the dedication ceremony during the Ryder Cup for golfer Byron Nelson at Oak Hill Country Club in Rochester, when Byron mentioned his friendship with me during his acceptance speech, and my dad nearly fell out of his chair; or taking my dad and nephew from their home in Rochester to nearby Buffalo for the Stanley Cup Finals, where the Stars won in 1999. But likely, the most meaningful moment was taking my dad and his brother, my uncle, Howard, to a weekend of festivities at the fiftieth anniversary of the NHL All-Star Game in Toronto in 2000, thanks to my dear friends, Alan White (CEO of PlainsCapital) and Bob Gainey (the former general manager of the Dallas Stars, currently the general manager of the Montreal Canadiens). It meant so much to them, as, ironically, my dad and his brother had gone with their dad (my grandfather) to Maple Leaf Gardens in Toronto over fifty years ago. Now, half a century later, I was able to give them a trip down memory lane. My dad and my uncle were like a couple of kids at Christmastime when I took them down to the locker room after the Heroes of Hockey Old-Timers Game, and they met hockey legends, including Henri Richard, Gordie Howe, Ted Lindsay, and Frank Mahovolich.

Some of the blessings that attend a career in the media are the good fortune to witness hundreds of great events, be there for so many memorable moments, and meet the newsmakers of the day—ultimate achievers in the athletic arena who set themselves apart by their sheer dedication, discipline, and dominance. To have witnessed their feats firsthand, learned from their mistakes, and been touched by their accomplishments has been a privilege that few get to savor. But the part I have cherished the most has been the journey with my father, and eventually, my own son. To have had the opportunity to introduce my dad to the very individuals he once introduced me to (even if from afar) as examples of commitment, character, and courage is simply priceless.

So, this book isn't about me. It's about my dad. It's about sports legends. It is also for my son, Doug, who later would get ample opportunities to be at my side and go where relatively few young men have gone before—looking up to the likes of John Elway and rubbing shoulders with soon-to-be legends like Wayne Gretzky. I remember taking Doug with me to do an interview with Pete Rose, when he was still playing. Pete also had his son with him at the time. Pete looked at me and said, "That's nice that you take your boy with you, but I bet he doesn't have a clue that the world he's growing up in isn't the normal world of most boys."

But all that would be meaningless to me if it were not for the stories and life lessons that my own dad shared with me over the years, using positive sports figures as word-picture illustrations of how I should live my own life. He knew I loved sports, so he knew I'd listen and hopefully learn from these real-life examples.

The convictions I hold and the values I cherish are Dad's gifts to me, any measurement of which far surpasses whatever experiences in sports I have been blessed to have. And believe me, those in themselves are rich. What I hope to do is pass along what I've been taught by my father and, in turn, what I've learned in seeing things for myself to my son. I am a sports guy, after all, a son who loves his father, and a father who loves his own son.

This book and the life lessons it offers are a testimony to my dad and a gift to my son and my daughter, as well as to anyone who can appreciate and savor the achievements and humanity of the following sports legends who are especially meaningful to me—people from whom I learned along the way to try and do it right.

I

LOU GEHRIG

CHARACTER

*Try not to become a man of success,
but rather try to become a man of value.*

—Albert Einstein

O f all the sports figures featured in this book, Lou Gehrig is one of two I never met. No chance of that: he passed away at age thirty-seven in 1941, about a decade before I was born.

My dad always talked about Lou Gehrig. He was Dad's favorite athlete, which makes perfect sense. Dad was big on character, and he was always talking about the Iron Horse. He liked the fact that Gehrig was not only well educated, a Columbia man, but that he was a humble person. You didn't have to be alive in the 1920s and 1930s to know that; you could see it and sense it in the many books and magazine articles that tell about his short life on earth—about how he played in 2,130 consecutive games, a record that stood for fifty-six years until Cal Ripken Jr. broke it in 1995, and how he died of a disease that would eventually be named after him.

Everyone knows about the "I consider myself the luckiest man on the face of the earth" speech that a dying Gehrig gave at home plate in front of a microphone at Yankee Stadium, bidding a heartfelt farewell to the world at large. No other moment in sports has equaled the authentic pathos of that moment, one that Gary Cooper so eloquently performed in the movie *The Pride of the Yankees*. It was at that time that Lou Gehrig proclaimed, without actually saying it himself (he would never have done such a thing), that he was a man of great value. A man of character. Those who knew him knew it.

Years ago while I was in New York City, I was browsing suits in a men's clothing store when I came across a two-by-three-foot framed portrait of the 1927 New York Yankees, still regarded by many as the greatest baseball team of all time. Why this photo happened to be in this clothing store, I'm not really sure. But I knew I wanted it. I told the store manager of my interest, and he ended up selling it to me along with the sweater I was purchasing. I was elated. The classic black-and-white photo was mine.

In the team photo, there are only twenty-four guys pictured. Three of them are sitting on the ground in front of the bench, then there's the middle row of guys sitting on the bench, and then there's the top row. Lou Gehrig is the fifth guy from the right in the top row, although you can barely see his face. He is largely obscured by one of his teammates, a slight smile forming on his lips, the look of someone semi-amused to be in the photo and making no attempt to force his full face into the picture. It's like he wants to remain partially hidden, letting his teammates hold center stage while he stays in the background.

That Gehrig pose seems to confirm everything I have heard about the man—one of the great players on perhaps the greatest team in baseball history, yet he can take or leave the attendant publicity.

Another quirk of the photo is what Babe Ruth is doing in the picture. He also is standing in the back row, apart from Gehrig, at the very right edge. Ruth is there, but he really isn't. He has his left hand on the shoulder of the teammate seated in front of him, but he's not looking at the camera. In fact, The Babe is the only one of the twenty-four players pictured not looking at the camera. Instead, he's looking off in the distance to one side, perhaps spotting someone or something that only he is distracted by.

Then, in contrast, there's Gehrig, the superstar out of the limelight, content to stay slightly out of the focus of the photo, almost like he's embarrassed about even being there in the first place, when perhaps he'd be more comfortable fielding grounders over at first base or taking extra batting practice before that afternoon's exhibition. He's like that quiet yet engaging favorite uncle of yours at the family reunion, shoehorned in the back of the combined-family pose, sneaking a peek over the shoulder of Cousin Jerry who's huddled shoulder to shoulder with wife Lucille, holding eighteen-month-old Jerry Jr.

Where Ruth basked on the front page, Gehrig tolerated it.

Dad loves that picture. It is worth the thousands of words my dad over the years has espoused on Lou Gehrig, once described by legendary sports columnist Jim Murray as "a Gibraltar in cleats."

Beginning in 1927, Gehrig and Ruth started to dominate baseball like no two teammates had ever dominated the game before or, arguably, since. Long before there were Mantle and Maris, there were Ruth and Gehrig, putting chase to and smashing baseball's single-season home run mark, with Ruth hitting sixty in 1927, while Gehrig tailed off late and ended up with forty-seven. Together, Ruth and Gehrig out-homered every other American League team except one.

Gehrig's numbers over the years were eye-popping. He *averaged* one hundred forty-seven runs batted in a year. For twelve consecutive seasons he batted .300 or better and on June 3, 1932, became the first American leaguer to hit four home runs in one game, barely missing a fifth. He won the Triple Crown in 1934 with a .363 batting average, forty-nine home runs and 165 runs batted in. Gehrig amassed more than four hundred total bases, five times in his career, compared to just twice for Ruth.

Speaking of Ruth, during a barnstorming trip to Japan in the mid-1930s, he broke off what had been a good relationship with Gehrig, supposedly miffed over a comment that Gehrig's mother had made about how Ruth's daughter dressed. The two legendary teammates refused to exchange words again until years later at Lou Gehrig Appreciation Day.

How does one appreciate Lou Gehrig? Consider that this son of German immigrants was the only one of four children to survive to adolescence. His mom, Christina, was forced to work three jobs to help make ends meet. That's because his father, Heinrich, always seemed to have trouble finding a job, and, at that, he often was in poor health.

Gehrig's own health took a turn for the worse in 1938, when his batting average fell below .300 for the first time since 1925. His strength was failing him, and the bland diet that doctors put him on to combat what had been diagnosed as a gallbladder problem only made him weaker. The Iron Horse stuck it out and tried to return for the 1939 season, but less than a month into the season he took himself out of the Yankees' lineup. On May 2, 1939, Babe Dahlgren took over at first base, not only ending Gehrig's 2,130-game playing streak, but also finishing off his playing career in the process.

Mayo Clinic doctors examined Gehrig, and this time they found that he had a rare degenerative muscle disease known as amyotrophic lateral sclerosis (ALS), later to be renamed "Lou Gehrig's Disease."

As a host of the Jerry Lewis Labor Day MDA Telethon for over a quarter of a century, I sadly learned and vividly witnessed what an insidious disease ALS is. And each time I'm introduced to a new patient, I am reminded of the horror that Lou Gehrig and those that followed were forced to endure, as the search for a cure continues even today.

When Gehrig, fighting back tears, gave his "luckiest man" speech before sixty-two thousand fans at Yankee Stadium on July 4, 1939, Ruth walked up to his long-time teammate, put his arm around him, and spoke into his ear the first words he had shared with him in five years. That December, Gehrig was elected to the Baseball Hall of Fame.

Even though his baseball career was over and his health was in a steady decline, Gehrig accepted an offer to perform community work that included working on New York's parole board to help troubled youths.

When I think of Gehrig, I remember taking my dad to Yankee Stadium in 1977. The first thing he said to me was, "There's first base, right where Lou Gehrig used to play." It was a *Field of Dreams* moment for both of us, in reverse.

On June 2, 1941, Gehrig passed away, his legacy as a man with a kind heart, a winning attitude, and a commitment to character secured for eternity. Years later when actor Edward Hermann was preparing to play the role of Gehrig for a TV movie, he said that in all of his research he could not find a "key" to Gehrig on which to peg his portrayal. "There was no strangeness, nothing spectacular about him," Hermann said. "As Eleanor Gehrig (Lou's widow) told me, he was just a square, honest guy." Just like my dad!

Dad's kind of guy. Mine too.

II

JESSE OWENS

DIGNITY

True dignity is never gained by place,
and never lost when honors are withdrawn.

—Philip Massinger

For years athletes have told us about how they've had to overcome adversity in their lives to get to where they are. With a straight face and a hint of somberness, many of our sporting role models regale us with heart-tugging stories about how they have persevered through tough contract negotiations or been coerced into having to represent their countries in some international competition that doesn't pay a million-dollar bonus.

Pity the superstar who has had to endure taunts of alleged steroid use or who has been stressed to the point of wondering how he can possibly feed his family on $7 million a year. Those are the hardships we hear about today, which sound so silly and trivial when you ponder the life and achievements of one Jesse Owens.

If you want to talk about hardship and make the leap over to adversity, then Owens is your man. Most athletes and sports fans under the age of forty have never even heard of Jesse Owens, either because he hasn't done any big endorsement deals lately or their knowledge of American sports history doesn't predate the invention of the DVD. There's a reason for the former—Owens has been dead more than twenty-five years. Besides, film footage of his exploits as perhaps the greatest American track athlete are of the old, herky-jerky, black-and-white variety lost among the dust-filled canisters stowed away in some musty warehouse, right next to the ark of the covenant.

Adversity? Try this on for size: born in 1913 in Oakville, Alabama, which in those days was hardly the ideal launching pad for black men looking to someday excel in a white man's sport, James Cleveland Owens was a sickly child. He suffered from chronic bronchial congestion and endured several bouts of pneumonia, at the time a killer for many folks.

Born into poverty that meant inadequate nutrition and clothing, among other of life's inconveniences for a family with almost no money, Owens by the age of seven was working in the cotton fields, tasked daily to pick a hundred pounds of the fluffy stuff.

When he was nine, his family moved to Cleveland, where his Southern accent led one teacher to believe that when the young Owens was giving his name as "J.C.," she thought he was saying "Jesse," and that's how James Cleveland—J.C.—became Jesse. Soon, though, Jesse was making a name for himself in ways that far transcended his upbringing. And he wasn't a sickly child anymore, either.

In high school he set or tied national records at 100 and 220 yards and in the long jump, then known as the "broad jump." Not a particularly good student, Owens had no trouble getting a scholarship to Ohio State to compete in track for the Buckeyes, and it was there in 1935 that he put on one of the greatest one-day performances in sports history.

Unable even to bend over and do a toe touch—the result of slipping and falling on his tailbone while running away with friends after pulling a prank—Owens, in the span of forty-five minutes at a meet in Ann Arbor, Michigan, set or tied four world records.

It went like this: at 3:15 p.m., he ran the 100-yard dash in a world-record-tying 9.4 seconds; at 3:25 p.m., making only one jump, he long-jumped twenty-six feet, eight and a quarter inches to set a world record that would hold up for twenty-five years; at 3:34 p.m., Owens ran the 220 in a world-record 20.3 seconds; finally, as the clock struck 4:00 p.m., he became the first person ever to break 23 seconds in the 220 low hurdles—his time of 22.6 seconds set a new world record.

The best was yet to come, and it would come on a world stage in front of an evil world dictator who knew a thing or two about creating adversity for others. Real adversity, the kind that tries a man's soul, not just his patience or his agent's bottom line.

The 1936 Summer Olympics will forever be known as "the Nazi Olympics," the ones in which Adolph Hitler's Nazis claimed that African Americans were "inferior non-humans," comprising a group of competitors the Nazis derided as "black auxiliaries" being unfairly used by the Americans. It wasn't an entirely hostile environment, though. Crowds in excess of one hundred thousand in Berlin's Olympic Stadium cheered on Owens as he dazzled anyone not wearing a Nazi uniform by winning four gold medals.

It had to be a spine-tingling phenomenon on two levels for Owens: on the one, experiencing the kind of thunderous applause and support that instantly sprouts goose bumps; on the other, the cold chill of being on stage, alone much of the time, in front of a malicious dictator avowed to rule the world and kill millions of those who didn't fit his definition of a master race. Clad in only a tank top and shorts much of the time, Owens must have shivered from the solitary nature of his sport, exposed on a world stage with all eyes upon him.

Through it all, he held his chin and head high, never reacting in any way to show disdain for his detractors or acquiescence to those who would shun him.

Those who were on Owens's side included fellow competitor Lutz Long, who with his long athletic build, blue eyes, and blond hair epitomized Hitler's obsession with establishing a master race. With Owens down to his last attempt at the long-jump qualifier following two fouls, Long introduced himself to Owens and then graciously suggested to the American that he draw himself a line a few inches behind the takeoff board so as to play it safe and not risk a disqualifying third foul.

Owens took Long's advice, made a successful qualifying jump on his final attempt, then went on to win the gold medal in the finals with a leap of twenty-six feet, five and a half inches to edge out Long, who was the first one to congratulate the new Olympic long-jump champion.

"It took a lot of courage for him to befriend me in front of Hitler," Owens later said. "You can melt down all the medals and cups I have, and they wouldn't be plating on the twenty-four-karat friendship I felt for Lutz Long at that moment. Hitler must have gone crazy watching us embrace."

This was seventy years ago. It's mind-boggling to think of the power of that Owens moment so long ago. Fifteen years after those games, there would be another powerful moment. It was 1951. The Harlem Globetrotters traveled to Germany to play at Berlin Olympic Stadium as part of the team's twenty-fifth anniversary celebration tour. Just prior to tipoff, a helicopter landed on the field, and out emerged Jesse Owens, returning to the stadium for the first time since his record-breaking Olympic performance. The crowd of over seventy-five thousand fans rose to their feet and cheered nonstop for fifteen minutes straight, as Jesse waved and walked around the entire perimeter of the stadium. Marques Haynes, arguably the greatest Globetrotter ever, would tell me years later that it was one of the most emotional moments he ever witnessed, topped off by German chancellor Konrad Adenauer addressing Owens and the crowd, saying, "Fifteen years ago the leader of our country refused to extend a hand of congratulations on your great accomplishments, so today, I'm honored to represent all of Germany and offer both hands to a great champion."

It's easy to be in awe of Jesse Owens, so much so that when I was in sixth grade, I chose to write a term paper on him. My parents had often talked about his greatness and grace both as a person and an athlete, so, because of my great love of sports, it was an easy decision to make. It was during the research of that term paper assignment that I learned what prejudice and racism were really all about.

When you watch those old films of Owens running, it's his posture that grabs your attention. His body is upright, his head held high, his upper body so still as he runs. It looks almost effortless, very similar to how future

Olympic gold medalist Michael Johnson would run. An expert no less qualified than Ruth Owens, Jesse's widow, would point out that uncanny similarity years later after seeing Johnson run. It's almost as if both Owens and Johnson were supremely self-conscious of their posture, keeping their backs straight and chins up as they raced toward the finish line.

Men of distinction. Regal, almost.

My good fortune to meet this remarkable man came in the mid-1970s. I was in Albany in upstate New York, my first full-time television job, working at the ABC affiliate, later to switch over to CBS. Having been asked to serve as the master of ceremonies at a high-school sports banquet, I was most excited because I knew Jesse Owens was going to be there too. So, I searched the library, found some old film of him, and dubbed it over to videotape. Then I was going to do an interview with him and put it all together as a feature on my sports show.

Jesse was quite soft-spoken and genteel, a perfect gentleman. Not a bad word to say about anybody. He conducted himself just like he ran: smoothly and with great bearing. Elegantly and with grace. That's exactly how he spoke when addressing the banquet audience, showing himself to be a man of great passion and vision. A perfect ambassador. The ultimate gentleman. It was a memorable night.

About six months later, I was again asked to serve as the emcee, this time at Albany State University, although I had no idea who the guest speaker was going to be.

That night, while walking across the school parking lot, I noticed this other man walking toward me. It was dusk, and the tall lights around the parking lot were on, making for a luminescent glow outside. So I couldn't make out who it was.

As he got closer to me, he suddenly said, "Hello," and then as he got even closer, he looked up with a smile and said, "Hey, how are you? It's Scott, isn't it?" It just about blew me away. It was Jesse Owens, and he had made an effort to remember my name a good six months after we had met for the first time in our lives. We had a wonderful time that night and kept in touch after that, although I never saw him again before he died. But it's a moment in time that I will never forget.

This figure I had read about in my history books and had seen in old sports films had taken on a role of a real person. A person who was one of the most humble, down-to-earth people I've ever met. A man who had overcome great adversity. A man who lived his life with great dignity.

III

BYRON NELSON

COMPASSION

Without a rich heart,
wealth is an ugly beggar.

—Ralph Waldo Emerson

For as long as I knew Byron Nelson—and that was half my life—one thing that I could always say about him was that everybody was attracted to him like a magnet. Not in the sense of a rock star–like celebrity in that he would get besieged by throngs, but in the sense that Byron was always an accommodating person with an engaging personality, like few people you had ever met in your life. He cared to know as much about you as you did about him.

Byron was a unique celebrity: totally unpretentious, unfailingly polite, a man of strong Christian convictions, and someone who could get right to the point in conversation without being blunt, brusque, or rude. One of the great ironies about Byron was that he was like a father to so many people, and yet he never had any children of his own. In that regard, being childless, Byron shared a fate with his longtime friend and golfing rival Ben Hogan, a fellow Fort Worth native.

For a number of years this compassionate man practically ruled the world of golf, yet was always quick with a helping hand or at least an encouraging word. At his final Nelson tournament, despite being well into his nineties and hobbled by age and growing infirmity, Byron rose out of his chair and onto his feet to greet everyone from tour favorites to relatively unknown golfers less than one-third his age. He extended a genuine sentiment of warmth that was an endless source of support to others with less than half the ability he had displayed in his prime.

While age and various things such as hip surgery had slowed him down physically, he remained as vibrant and cognizant as he ever was—sharp as a tack and on top of what's going on in the world, especially on the golf course—until the day he died at age ninety-four. His Byron Nelson Classic (or Championship, as it's now called) has been around for almost forty years, and it has grown to be one of the most popular stops for PGA Tour pros.

Byron's tournament was more than just an event in his name—it was an event at which he was honored. It became a tradition that Byron would sit in his box in the grandstands overlooking the eighteenth green and personally greet the golfers as they came off the course. And most of the time, it was not just superficial, polite chitchat. Byron would take the time to ask players specific questions about how they played, and he would listen to everything they said and then offer encouragement or even advice, if it was solicited. That was Lord Byron. It is no wonder that up to his final days, Nelson retained a strong kinship with scores of veteran pros, most notably Ken Venturi, Tom Watson, and Ben Crenshaw. It was not uncommon for any golfer, from a Phil Mickelson to a struggling young pro, to receive a personal note from Byron, lending encouragement and support. When Tiger Woods was just a teenager, Byron took the time to seek him out and encouraged him, lent support, and reminded him of the importance of good conduct, all the while assuring him he'd someday be a great success. Byron told young Tiger to call him anytime he needed a listening ear. No doubt, Woods took advantage of Mr. Nelson's offer more than once. Aside from 2006, when Tiger's dad passed away shortly before the tournament, Woods has faithfully returned to the Nelson Championship out of respect for his longtime mentor and friend every year since turning pro.

The first time I met Byron was at the 1980 PGA Championship at Oak Hill Country Club in Rochester, New York. It was pro-am day, and as I was walking along the sidewalk not far from the clubhouse, I saw him standing off to the side. Because no one was there with him at the time, I took it upon myself to amble over and introduce myself. I was scheduled to do a live broadcast for the noon news in about twenty minutes, so I figured this would be a perfect opportunity to get an interview with a living legend. However, there was no assurance the enthusiasm to have him on my show would be mutual. Obviously, he had no clue who I was, and it dawned on me that he might have been standing alone for the sole intent of being left alone for a short while.

Byron was terrific with me. When I asked him if he would do the live interview, he asked me where I was going to be when I did it. I told him, and he said he would be there and would be glad to do it. What struck me in all this was how mild mannered he was, and yet he had such a presence about him. I guess you could call it compassionate charisma, as there was really no sense of distance involved. He was close to seventy at the time, yet his responsiveness was that of a much younger man, full of verve and able to answer questions with depth and knowledge. He took such great care to answer all of my questions and then asked if I had everything I needed. I'm sure he would have stayed longer and answered more questions had I asked. There's that "compassion" again. But that was Byron with his caring and concerned commitment to others.

Byron knew what it was like to be behind the microphone, having served as a television analyst with his dear friend and legendary sportscaster, Chris Schenkel, for two decades. He began his broadcast career close to half a century ago in 1957. He and Schenkel were stationed at the sixteenth green at Augusta, covering the Masters. By the time the Masters teed off the following year, Byron and Chris were anchoring the prestigious tournament from the coveted eighteenth green. Byron was a natural—factual, folksy, and familiar to the TV audience. He became so popular and well-respected that he served as an analyst for all three networks—ABC, CBS, and NBC—during a twenty-year stint in the booth.

One thing that disappoints me when talking about Byron—and the likes of Hogan, Sam Snead, et al.—is that today's young golfer or golf fan really doesn't know who Byron is or what he accomplished, both as a golfer and a self-made farmer-turned-businessman. I have read in recent years how today's young superstars in various sports can't name or even tell you about the superstars of yesteryear in their sports, even ones who might have competed just twenty-five or thirty years ago. That boggles my mind.

Growing up in the '60s, when the current sports stars included the likes of Mickey Mantle, Willie Mays, Johnny Unitas, and Gordie Howe, I would not only give you chapter and verse on those guys, I could also do it for the previous generation's stars, such as Babe Ruth, Ty Cobb, Sammy Baugh, Ben Hogan, Jesse Owens—all those guys. And I was able to know all this without benefit of the Internet, an iPod, or a BlackBerry. I'd be interested to do a random survey of today's young star athletes and ask what they can tell me about, say, Larry Bird. Or George Brett. Or Bobby Orr. Or Walter Payton. Ditto for young sports fans. Wanna stump a young pro golfer or golf fan? Ask him or her what golfer won consecutive U.S. Opens in the late 1980s (Curtis Strange) or what legendary women's golfer, who's still young enough to be only in her forties, won five consecutive LPGA events as a rookie in the late 1970s (Nancy Lopez). Imagine how bewildered this young golfer/golf fan would be if you were to run names such as Palmer, Nicklaus, and Trevino past him or her, let alone Hogan, Snead, and Nelson. Most would be clueless.

Let me enlighten you a little bit about Byron Nelson. Before leaving full-time golf after the 1946 season, Nelson forged one of the greatest careers in professional golf. He could, as they say, shoot lights out on the golf course. For the record, Nelson twice won the Masters as well as two PGA Championships and a U.S. Open. Fifty-two official PGA Tour event wins in all.

His most memorable year was 1945, when he won an incredible total of eighteen tour events, including a streak of eleven straight that remains to this day arguably the most unassailable sports record in the books. When Tiger Woods won six in a row a few years back, there was talk that Woods had a good chance to catch Byron. But face it, as great a player as Woods was and is, his achievement put him only halfway to breaking Byron's record streak. Like they say, that's a record that will probably never be broken.

Years later, to celebrate the fiftieth anniversary of Byron's streak of "11 Straight," the Four Seasons Resort and Club (site of Byron's tournament) hosted an event, inviting a team from each of those eleven clubs to participate in a three-day tournament. Byron asked Schenkel to serve as the master of ceremonies for the occasion. Unfortunately, Chris, who was in failing health at the time, had to pass on the request. Byron then called me and asked if I would fill in. Obviously, I was most honored, first to be asked by Byron and secondly, to replace a familiar voice like Chris Schenkel, whom I had grown up listening to. Teams from most of the clubs Nelson had played and tournaments Nelson had won traveled to Texas to renew old acquaintances and forge new ones. But the highlight of the entire affair was witnessing the reactions and learning of the relationships between Byron and the folks representing the very clubs at which he had made history half a century ago. It was, indeed, good stuff. And Byron was like a kid on Christmas morning, reliving what had taken place fifty years ago.

And yet, Byron was most proud of his annual tournament and the good that it does for young people. The incredible work and continued commitment of the Salesmanship Club of Dallas helped Byron raise close to $100 million, representing roughly 10 percent of the total monies raised by tour events for PGA charities (more than any other tournament). "It's the best thing that's ever happened to me in golf," said Byron. "Better than winning the Masters or the U.S. Open or eleven in a row, because it helps people." That was Byron Nelson—proud of his golf game but even more revered for his humble, benevolent, compassionate ways. Days before his death, Byron learned that backers had received sufficient support from the House and the Senate for him to be presented with the Congressional Gold Medal for his philanthropic endeavors. Only 138 people have ever received the honor, beginning with George Washington. Only four other athletes have ever been honored: Jackie Robinson, Jesse Owens, Roberto Clemente, and Joe Louis. Byron would have been the first not to receive it posthumously.

Byron was a good man who was kind to everyone he met. In that regard, he had a lot of Will Rogers in him. I honestly don't know why, but he took an interest in me from the time I moved to the DFW area, which was just months after I had met him at Oak Hill. He invited me to his house on several occasions. When his wife Louise passed away in 1985, I was asked to be an honorary pallbearer at her funeral. Any time I ever needed him on the air, he always said yes. When my wife, Carole, met him for the first time, the words she later used to describe him were "so kind and cute." Of all the athletes and sports personalities she's met, Byron remains her all-time favorite. Byron adored her as well.

Then there's the ranch in Roanoke. Byron had always wanted to play golf until he made enough money to buy some farmland in Texas and live the rest of his life there with Louise. The ranch house, which basically is the same modest home he built back in the 1940s, used to be way out, miles away from both Fort Worth and Dallas. But with the encroaching development over the years, with the likes of Alliance Airport and Texas Motor Speedway, his ranch has become part of the greater metroplex. His home sits atop a hill that you can see from the road, Old Highway 114 (which now bears the name Byron Nelson Boulevard). Most of the traffic has now been diverted to the new, widened Highway 114.

Byron and his second wife, Peggy (who would have celebrated their twentieth anniversary in November 2006), lived a Norman Rockwell–like existence out at the ranch. It's a two-story farmhouse surrounded by acres of fields, a few trees, and two or three man-made ponds next to a little cottage of about six hundred square feet that Byron built years ago. He and Louise would sit at the cottage and just enjoy each other's company while watching the sunset. In recent years, Peggy had fixed up the cottage (sitting room, kitchen, and bathroom) because it had gotten a bit run-down. It's a trip back in time.

There is a wood shop across from the house where Byron liked to go and tinker. Carpentry was one of his passions, and he built many pieces of furniture for the house as well as items he gave away to friends. Just weeks before his passing, Byron was busy making wood carvings for America's Ryder Cup Team. There are still a couple of tractors on the property, although it had been years since Byron had been on one of them—plowing soil, or baling hay, or performing one of a dozen other duties he used to have as a true-to-life farmer.

It was always a treat to visit Byron and Peggy at their ranch. The normal routine was to stop at Babe's (about a seven iron from his home), pick up some of the best chicken Texas has to offer, and head to the ranch for some fun, food, fellowship, and a night of storytelling second to none. It was like visiting your grandfather as a kid. In the back entrance to the house, there is a small study with a desk. Lots of pictures and memorabilia hanging on the walls. All from a gentler time. Point something out to Byron, and he always had a tale to tell you, rich in detail. All around the house are these poignant little sayings, many written in crochet, and a lot of them with a Christian theme to them. There is a little living room with a fireplace, and here you can find mementos from the Masters and other major events that Byron had competed in.

Byron was only thirty-four when he retired from golf. He and Louise shared almost forty years together at the ranch before she passed away less than a month after a second stroke. When Louise died, Byron was close to a broken man, and being in his seventies really showed. But a year later, he married Peggy, a woman over three decades younger than Byron, and to see the revitalization that took place in Byron with Peggy at his side was nothing short of remarkable. Peggy is a tremendously well-rounded person, a terrific writer and artist, and someone with business savvy who helped guide Byron as much as she loved him. Five minutes rarely went by in conversation that Byron wasn't saying something special about Peggy.

It's ironic that Byron would die less than forty-eight hours after the conclusion of the 2006 Ryder Cup. For it was at the Royal Birkdale course in Southport, England, that Byron proudly captained the U.S. Ryder Cup team to victory over Great Britain in 1965. I'll never forget being at Oak Hill Country Club to cover the 1995 Ryder Cup. Nelson had been invited that week to be honored with a tree dedicated to him at the thirteenth hole, a long par-five. This is how Oak Hill honors its legends, and it was Byron's turn. Up on a hill at the thirteenth is a cluster of big oak trees, and on each tree there is a bronze plaque in recognition of a particular golfing great.

There were something like two or three hundred people gathered around for the ceremony, all seated in chairs that had been brought out for this grand event. My dad accompanied me because he lives so close to Rochester. And once again, Byron's tremendous compassion for others came through.

I was sitting there with my dad when it was Byron's turn to get up and speak, to thank Oak Hill for the honor. He reminisced about this and that, telling some great stories, and as he got toward the end of his speech, he said, "I've got some people here from Dallas and Fort Worth who came along to join me for this." After he mentioned various people, he said, "And I gotta say a special hello to my good friend and one of my favorite sportscasters, Scott Murray, who's always been a great friend."

I'm sure that Byron in large part said it because he knew my dad was there with me and that it would be a nice way to pay homage to father and son. I thought my dad was going to lose it right there, and he leaned over to me and whispered, "Hey, Scott, he's talking about you." I said, "Yeah. Isn't that nice, Dad." As kind a gesture as it was, I was more thrilled for my dad than for me.

Again, we had come full circle from the time in 1968 when I was in high school and my dad took me to Oak Hill that June to watch the U.S. Open, which Lee Trevino won. Dad was helping me get autographs from guys like Palmer, Nicklaus, and Player. I'll never forget when I received my subscription to *Sports Illustrated* the following week. On the cover, there's a photo of Dad, me, and about a thousand other people behind the eighteenth green at Oak Hill, watching as Trevino finished off the victory that made him an instant worldwide sensation. Twenty-seven years later, Dad and I were back at Oak Hill, this time with Byron Nelson, watching the Ryder Cup.

Over the years, I have had the opportunity to emcee numerous events at which Byron was the honored guest. And without question, on each occasion, my introduction for him was always the same. Following a brief history of his incredible career, I'd simply conclude by saying, "The best thing I can share with you about Byron is that if I didn't have a father of my own whom I love and respect as much as I do, this is the man I would choose to take my father's place. That, I hope, will tell you what I think of Byron Nelson." With Byron's passing, I will never have that opportunity again. But I will forever cherish our special friendship. Without ever giving me a lesson on life, he taught me volumes on how to live, simply by watching and learning from the caring, committed, and compassionate way he lived his own life. Sadly, there will never be another Byron Nelson, yet thankfully, he will always be remembered. As 1964 U.S. Open champion Ken Venturi often said, "You can always argue who was the greatest player, but Byron is the finest gentleman the game has ever known."

IV

BEN HOGAN

COURAGE

Courage is going from failure to failure without losing enthusiasm.

—Winston Churchill

It's almost impossible to talk about Byron Nelson without bringing Ben Hogan into the conversation, and vice versa. Their two lives are about as connected as any two men's could be in terms of their love of golf, their roots, their decades-long acquaintanceship starting when they were kids, and their respective impacts on the game of golf. They were both born in 1912, and both cut their teeth on golf at Glen Garden Country Club in Fort Worth, starting out as caddies.

Beyond that, they are about as opposite in personality and public-relations prowess as two men of like backgrounds could be. They are as different as salt and pepper. Nelson has always been accessible, talkative, gracious, forever willing to lend a hand or dispense a golf tip. Hogan, who passed away in 1997, wasn't like that—at least not in public. For much of the last forty years of his life, he was somewhat of a recluse, a man of few words who rarely smiled in public, and who, while polite like Nelson, never went out of his way to meet strangers or part with much warmth.

Friends close to Hogan will paint a different picture, saying, "No, you have it all wrong. Ben was just a shy guy who in private with friends could be quite funny and engaging, even somewhat of a jokester." Fine, but that's the side most people never saw of Hogan, when they saw him at all. It is fair to judge public figures as you see them out and about, and there never was a chance that Hogan would be mistaken for a Will Rogers wannabe. Many would say he was cold, plain and simple. And that cold, abrupt, to-the-point personality could occasionally translate into hurtful words. Like the time a young, blue-collar pro named Arnold Palmer, in the locker room at Augusta

National, overheard Hogan ask another player, "How the hell did Palmer get an invitation to the Masters?" The year was 1958. Palmer never confronted Hogan about his remarks. He simply went out and won the first of his four green jackets.

All that said, Hogan is one of the most intriguing people I've ever met. And yes, he could be intimidating. Ask him any question and you would get one of two things: a brief answer that was straight to the point or no answer at all—just a stare. "Yeah," his supporters would say, "that's just Ben being Ben, and it's not because he doesn't like you. It's because he wants to give you a thoughtful answer and is still thinking about it."

My dad used to tell me about Ben Hogan a lot. I remember as a kid watching the movie *Follow the Sun,* starring Glenn Ford as Hogan. It was overtly sentimental and maybe a bit too sweet, but still it had an impact on me. More than anything else, what the black-and-white film accomplished was its depiction of the courage of Hogan, the man who was a notorious hack in his early years as a pro golfer, determined to work on his game over and over and over until he got it right, which he did, particularly, on the high side of forty years.

More vivid, though, is the courage that Hogan displayed to a watching world as he gutted out a comeback after a horrific auto crash on a fog-bound road in West Texas. This, in the middle of the night while traveling (cross-country) with wife, Valerie, on the passenger side. At first, fearing for Hogan's life, doctors upgraded Hogan's prognosis to such that while he would live, he likely would not be able to walk ably again, certainly not well enough to continue playing golf, let alone at a pro-tour caliber. But Bantam Ben proved them all wrong, painfully and persistently working his way back to become a golfer better than ever, once again winning majors and stunning everyone—except himself.

Many people who follow sports, including sportswriters, will tell you that TV sportscasters aren't really journalists at all—that we just put a happy face on sports coverage and spend the bulk of our time schmoozing with sports figures, trying to be their friends, or at least trying to get them to like us. That's a pretty broad brushstroke, when the truth is actually something quite a bit different. In reality, we don't treat sports figures as marks to get chummy with, and even when we try to get an interview, we don't always succeed. Case in point: Ben Hogan.

Through most of the 1980s, it was generally conceded in and around DFW that Hogan was, by his decree, off-limits to the media. He and his wife, Valerie, childless like Byron and Louise, lived in a fairly ritzy part of west Fort Worth known as Westover Hills, just about a drive and an eight iron away from Ben's favorite daily destination, Shady Oaks Country Club. He would show up for lunch almost every day to sit with the same group of pals and often hit some balls out on the practice range, occasionally dispensing swing tips to the aspiring tour-pro likes of Kris Tschetter and Tom Byrum.

In the spring of 1989, though, Hogan for some reason—some claim it was health problems that might have given him a greater sense of his own mortality—came out of his shell and started accepting interviews with the media. As I remember it, the first one to somehow get Hogan to consent to a sit-down interview was the *Fort Worth Star-Telegram* and, soon after, *The Dallas Morning News,* and both ran big pieces featuring Hogan that May, around the time of the Byron Nelson Classic and the Colonial.

That was the apparent opening I was looking for, so I immediately called the Hogan Company, where Ben still kept an office, and asked his assistant, Doxie Williams, if Hogan would agree to an on-air interview with me. She said she didn't know if Mr. Hogan would do it but that she would check with him to see if he would at least agree to a meeting with me to discuss it. Doxie called me back a little later and said that Mr. Hogan would be happy to meet with me, but it would have to be at nine o'clock the next morning.

The next day, trying to put forth my own brand of Hogan-esque cour-age, I dressed in a nice suit and showed up at Hogan's office about fifteen minutes early. He was already there, and when my time came to meet with him, Doxie walked me into his office and introduced me. He remembered me from when I had first met him sometime earlier at a public function, saying, "Scott, it's good to see you again. What can I do for you?"

That's when I told him that I would appreciate the opportunity to bring a TV crew over and tape an interview with him. I said, "I'd love to reminisce with you. Byron is a good friend, and I've done some things on TV with Byron over the years and would love to do something with you because you come out of the same era." Something like that.

It went over like a lead balloon. Politely but bluntly, Hogan informed me that while he appreciated the invitation, he wasn't doing any interviews, at least not any on camera. He then pointed to a door across his office and told me that behind that door was a closet full of golf balls and photos and other memorabilia that had been sent to him with requests for him to sign them. "Everybody wants something, and I'll get to them when I get to them, but I'm just too busy right now." It was obvious that he wasn't going to do the interview, and he didn't.

It was a disappointment made no less stinging when he then asked, "Is there any other way I can help you?" In fact, there was. I pulled out a photo I had had taken of me with him and Byron at the first Fort Worth Hall of Fame induction ceremony two years earlier. When I asked if he would sign it (Byron already had), he said he would gladly do it and then asked me what I wanted him to write on it. "Anything you'd like to, Mr. Hogan," I replied.

He must have taken a good five minutes. When he got to the part where he actually started signing his name, the first thing that came to mind when he had formed the "B" was, *Hey, it looks just like the "B" you see written on his signature golf clubs.* So methodical. After he had finished, he said to me, "I've been watching you a long time on TV. You do a great job, and I enjoy seeing you. I know you do a lot of things around town."

In fact, I do, and being persistent, told him that I happened to be on the board at Cook Children's Medical Center and that Mrs. Hogan was one of the founders of the Jewel Charity Ball, which benefits Cook Children's Hospital. So, there was that connection. But even that wasn't going to get me an interview with him. My mention of that led to more conversation, which led to something else, and before you knew it I had been there a long time.

Somewhere in all of this, he told me that those who want something bad enough will succeed at what they do, and those who don't want it bad enough—you can just tell. Hogan personified "wanting it bad enough." He wanted it bad enough to overcome the hellish moment in childhood when he, at age nine, was supposedly in the room at the time his father committed suicide by shooting himself. He wanted it bad enough to keep working at the game when Nelson was consistently beating him at golf, either as a boy or as a young touring pro in his twenties and early thirties. He wanted it bad enough to come back from a horrible auto wreck that nearly killed him and Valerie one dark, misty night on a Texas road. He wanted it bad enough to overcome all that and a wild duck hook when he was a young pro to refine his game and become one of the game's greatest ballstrikers. Talk about courageous.

His record is incredible: he won more than sixty PGA Tour events and numerous major championships, including the Masters, the U.S. Open, and the British Open all in 1953, a year's feat considered to be on the level of Bobby Jones's Grand Slam of 1930 and Nelson's eighteen victories in 1945.

As Ben and I neared the end of our conversation in his office that May morning, he finally said, "Well, I've got to get to lunch," and for a second I thought, *Oh, man, he's going to ask me to go to lunch with him.* Foolish me. Then he said, "I just want you to know I enjoyed having you stop by today." That's when I realized I was not going to have lunch with him that day. There would also be no TV interview. I had lots of great notes, but they don't work on television.

As I turned around to leave, I saw one of those big red, white, and blue Hogan Tour golf bags standing against a wall, and I said, "You see a lot of those on tour." Just like that, as though he was looking for an opening to try and give me something, even though he had said no to an interview, he responded in a giving tone:

"Do you need one of those?"

"No, sir. That's fine."

"Do you have a golf bag? We need to get you one of those."

I said no again, but it was obvious he would not hear of it. He said he planned to talk to the company president to tell him that he wanted me to get one of those bags. I really didn't think much about that after I left, but about a week later I got a call asking me where I wanted to have the golf bag delivered, and I said I really couldn't accept it because it went against my station's no-gifts policy, which said that we weren't allowed to accept gifts valued at twenty-five dollars or more. Whoever it was that called then said, "This is a gift from Mr. Hogan himself and not from the company, and he's giving it to you as a gesture of his friendship."

At that point, it would have been more awkward not accepting the golf bag than taking it. I let my superiors know what was happening and why, and they said it would be best, all things considered, that I accept the bag. To this day I have it.

Still, despite my perseverance, I never did get that interview. It could be he just didn't want to be on camera. But I recalled as I left that I did get to see a softer side of Mr. Hogan than I'd ever seen before. There seemed to be a more trusting side than when I initially walked in. My major was psychology, and I've tried to psychoanalyze him fifteen million ways, but all I can come up with is that perhaps he had some real, hidden issues as the result of his childhood.

Hogan was such a perfectionist, and that might have worked against him in the eyes of some. Being as focused as he was, first on his legendary golf game and later on the success of his company, he could almost be mistaken as rude or impolite. Obviously, he was a driven man. Sure, he had some guys helping him when he started the Hogan Company back in the 1950s, when he was still playing a few tournaments a year, but he was so much more hands-on with that company than just a celebrity who lent his name to it.

One time I was emceeing the Colonial champions' dinner and was sitting down at one end of the head table, right next to Hogan. Turns out I wasn't there by accident. He carried on a conversation with me all night. At one point Valerie came over to me and said, "Are you doing all right? Ben really enjoys you. I think he feels very comfortable with you sitting up here." She was right. He did seem to be at ease. I sensed that he trusted me, and I was pleased and honored that we were able to connect like that.

Years later, it would have been late 1995 or early 1996, I got a call from Colonial asking me if I would emcee a special dinner they were going to have for Mr. Hogan, at which time they would dedicate a statue to him that they were erecting on the club's premises. Because of his health issues, they couldn't yet commit to an exact date, but they asked if I would stay flexible with my schedule. "No problem," I said.

Finally, the club selected a specific date, but just three days before the dinner, the event had to be postponed due to Mr. Hogan's failing health. Colonial hoped to hold it within the next thirty days. But it never came to pass. Hogan passed away before they could ever formally dedicate the statue to him, although today it stands proudly at the entrance to Colonial Country Club.

For close to twenty years, I've served as one of the starters at the first tee during the Colonial tournament. During tournament time, a day doesn't go by that I don't respectfully revere the great names on the bronze wall of champions. And there, more than any other, is the name Ben Hogan, the man I never captured on camera but will always stand in awe of for his courage.

V

MIKE ERUZIONE

AND THE

1980 USA OLYMPIC HOCKEY TEAM

BELIEF

*To accomplish great things,
we must not only act, but also dream;
not only plan, but also believe.*

—Anatole Franc

There are a handful of events, maybe two, in our lives that we can point to as so memorable, so riveting, so life-changing that we can remember exactly where we were and what we were doing when those events took place. The Kennedy assassination. Man walking on the moon. *The Challenger* explosion. September 11, 2001, and the attack on the World Trade Center.

In the world of sports, there's the "Miracle on Ice" of February 1980, when a bunch of peach-fuzzed college players shocked the world and the vastly favored Russian hockey team by defeating the Soviets at Lake Placid, New York, en route to winning the Olympic gold medal.

I have no trouble remembering where I was and what I was doing that day. I was on ice. Actually, I was on snow, standing outside the arena as the Americans were defeating the Soviet national team, 4–3, in an upset considered to this day to be perhaps the greatest sports upset of all time. That says a lot when you also consider Jets over Colts in Super Bowl III and later that calendar year—in a remarkable continuing tale of two cities—Mets over Orioles in baseball's World Series. Let's also not forget N.C. State over Houston in the 1983 Final Four, Georgetown over Villanova two years later, or Buster Douglas over Mike Tyson.

The Miracle on Ice, which culminated in the United States' eventual victory over Finland two days later to wrap up the gold medal, still takes the cake. The victory over the Soviets sent a chill up and down my spine, literally, as I, like I said, was outside the arena on what was a very cold day. Why was I, a credentialed journalist, on the outside looking in? I had decided to share my pass with both my producer assistant, Peter, and cameraman,

John. We took turns watching the game, with Peter going inside to see the first period, John the second, and me to take in what would prove to be the pivotal third period.

From start to finish, it was an unforgettable game. I tell you that just in case you didn't get to see the game either in person or shown a little later on a tape-delayed basis by ABC Sports, or if you happened to miss the 2004 movie *Miracle* starring Kurt Russell as coach Herb Brooks.

The third period was an incredibly tense period of hockey. When the game ended with the Americans winning on the strength of Mike Eruzione's tie-breaking goal with exactly ten minutes left in the game—precisely midway through the third period—the "no cheering in the press box" rule was clearly violated by many journalists. Some of them were from other countries and secretly hoping the great Soviets would be taken down.

During each period, the two of us who stayed outside in our three-man rotation—although we could peek through the windows and see people moving about in the foyer—kept up with the game as best we could. We could feel the vibrations and hear the roar of the crowd from time to time, assuming each time that something good was happening for the American team. At times, I swear, we could even feel the building shaking, and it was one of those moments that we knew we were living a part of genuine American sports history.

One of the funniest parts about the whole experience came at the end of the first period, although neither John nor I were laughing about it at the time. After the first period ended, we noticed much of the crowd spilling out into the foyer, most to hit the concessions or at least hit the bathroom. John and I kept waiting and waiting as we watched hundreds of people walk by. Still, no Peter. We waited a few more minutes, but our string bean of a producer—Peter stood about six foot six and couldn't have weighed more than about 150 pounds—was still a no-show. When was he going to come out, and when were the rest of us going to get our chance to go inside?

Peter finally came out, but not without first teasing us with one of those peeking-around-the-corner-with-a-big-foolish-grin types of looks.

No one embodied that whole experience better than Mike Eruzione, the diminutive captain of the U.S. team, as voted on by his teammates. There's a lot about Eruzione that reminds me of Rudy, or at least Sean Astin's portrayal of Dan "Rudy" Reuttiger in the movie *Rudy*. Astin does an uncanny job of showing toughness and a bit of swagger mixed with adolescent-type enthusiasm, almost like he's still a kid trying to play a sport dominated by young men about to fully mature.

Eruzione had a lot of that in him back in 1980. He was not the best skater on the team, nor was he the best stickhandler or the obvious go-to guy when a goal was needed in a pinch. What he was was resilient and wise, someone able to catch on quickly to what Brooks was trying to do with the American players. That was to make them the best team they could be and not just an all-star collection of the best individual talent available.

The most enduring image of Eruzione is him alone atop the gold-medal podium at the medal ceremony, motioning for all his teammates to join him up there to share in the moment. There was nothing staged about that moment, the spontaneity of which added the perfect exclamation point to what had been a remarkable athletic achievement.

It's no wonder that Eruzione has had a long and successful second career in the limelight, commanding large speaking fees, as he travels the country to speak to groups about the power of dreams. It is to believe in yourself and to believe in a cause that allows you to transcend your own interests and what you can accomplish on your own. Eruzione epitomized the kind of player Herb Brooks was looking for. Brooks opted not to go with just the best players in making an all-star team, but in finding the right mix of players to give his team the blue-collar workmanship and chemistry it would need to have a chance at beating the big, bad Soviets.

Brooks believed in his players, and, in turn, those like Eruzione believed in themselves. Together as a team, their whole surpassed the sum of their parts.

I got a chance to interview Eruzione after the Finland game, long before he became a popular motivational speaker commanding twenty to thirty thousand per public appearance. Eruzione epitomized the Italian guy from the Northeast in the way he spoke with that classic "youse guys" type of talk that can be quite endearing. Where those guys are typically more gregarious than gracious, they all have a little bit of the latter.

Sometime in the aftermath of that gold-medal victory against Finland, an interview I did with Eruzione, with the American team gathered around him, somehow made its way around the world, picked up by a satellite link. Folks elsewhere around the country called my parents in Spencerport to tell them how their son was on TV, being Johnny-on-the-spot for a great Olympic moment. As proud parents often do, my folks treasure that video.

My dad was able to get a real kick out of this in more ways than one—as an American-hockey fan as well as father to a son who got to be there, even though it meant practically freezing my head off for two-thirds of the game while standing out in the snow.

I wouldn't have missed it for the world.

Long before the 1980 Miracle, my dad had told me all about that 1960 Olympic hockey team at Squaw Valley, the one that had been the last U.S. team to win Olympic gold. Brooks appears in the team picture, although the picture was taken prematurely, for Brooks would end up being the last player cut from the team. That ultimately denied him the gold medal he coveted as a player but would earn twenty years later as a coach. Poetic justice.

As for Eruzione, the 1980 Olympic gold medal would be the apex of his on-ice hockey career. But it was enough to last a lifetime. Everything about him reeked of grit and determination, the kind of guy who just could not be denied. Over the years, I have bumped into him at various events and shared with him further adventures in chitchat, and he has never ceased to exhibit the boyish enthusiasm that much of the world was witness to in 1980.

As for that cold, cold night in Lake Placid, when USA skated to that 4–3 victory over the Soviets, the one thing I still wonder about to this day is what happened to John and Peter during the third period, after I had finally gotten a chance to go inside to see the game. When the game was over and I came back outside, I could not find them anywhere. I have always questioned their claim that they were indeed outside the whole time.

Here's what I think; instead of cooling their heels, literally, outside, they made their way across the street to the Woodshed, a cozy little pub that we had come to know and love during our three-week stay in Lake Placid. It was the perfect place to go if you wanted to warm your cockles and rub shoulders with other folks who preferred the creature comforts of a warm and dry pub to a cold and snowy spot outside the arena. Which is fine with me, because to this day I always get a warm feeling from the memories of being outside the arena before finally getting my rinkside seat, as sports history unfolded no more than the length of a hockey stick from me. Without question, it was the most magical and memorable moment of my entire sportscasting career, demonstrating the true miracle of what can be achieved by simply believing in oneself.

VI

DAVID ROBINSON

INSPIRATION

Learn as if you were going to live forever.
Live as if you were going to die tomorrow.

—Mahatma Gandhi

T ake a good look at David Robinson and you see a modern-day Adonis. Handsome, clean-cut, tall (okay, very tall), and broad shouldered, with a ramrod-straight posture, a smile that melts, and a sculpted body that is muscular yet lean. He is a Naval Academy graduate and a former NBA superstar who won the league's MVP Award in 1995, and in 1999 and 2003 he was a "Twin Towers" partner with Tim Duncan of the San Antonio Spurs teams that won NBA titles.

By all accounts on the court and off, David Robinson appears the ultimate man, the high-performance, head-held-high warrior who made it a daily ritual to eat his three squares, all of his spinach, drink his milk, and push himself away from the table when his mom stuck a home-baked, high-calorie dessert in front of him.

It is okay to say this, to admit one's admiration of his fellow man for his commitment to himself, his body, and his mission to push himself to succeed at the highest level of his sport—all without ever losing the sense of who he is and why he is here, where he is going and how he plans to get there. In David Robinson's case, so much about him was almost too good to be true, starting with the lean yet rippled physique, glistening under sweat ten minutes into an NBA basketball game, getting up and down the court like a gazelle one moment, banging bodies against opponents the size of mini-aircraft carriers the next.

David Robinson (and for all I know this is still true) had the look of the ultimate, consummate athlete, the kind of superman who could run like the wind and knock out three-minute miles while carrying a scaled-down planet Earth on one shoulder: part Adonis, part Atlas, part Mercury.

Get this: he is unfailingly polite, too, with a wonderful sense of humor and a knowledge of so many things—something of a Renaissance man who is capable of dazzling you as much with his personality, intellect, and boldly professed faith in Jesus Christ as with his fancy footwork in the lane, his power moves to the hoops, and his uncanny ability to search out opponents' shots and swat them away before they reach their apex, let alone the basket.

My dad loved to talk about the Naval Academy and would marvel at Robinson for his focus and direction. "It's Roger Staubach all over again," Dad would tell me.

Too good to be true? Not exactly. Robinson has his warts, only most of us don't know what they are. In March 2003, even before Robinson had officially retired from the NBA, league commissioner David Stern announced that from that day forward, winners of the NBA Community Assist Award would receive the "David Robinson" instead. It would be inscribed, "Following the standard set by NBA Legend David Robinson, instead who improved the community piece by piece."

Robinson is the king of the court among sports figures who are philanthropists. Unlike many of his peers, Robinson doesn't just lend his name to charities or slice off a small percentage of a bloated salary to give to charities or causes because his agent says it's the right thing to do to nurture his PR image. Where others like him create foundations as tax shelters, Robinson has taken a hands-on, passionate role in proactively doing things to help other people.

The Carver Academy in downtown San Antonio is testament to David and Valerie Robinson's philanthropic efforts. They donated $11 million to the Academy named after the legendary botanist George Washington Carver. It's a school for inner-city children of elementary-school age who are being given a hand up in life. They have access to a strong academic program that includes small classes, activities geared toward experiencing leadership, and a family-like environment based on Judeo-Christian principles such as integrity, faith, and discipline.

The Robinsons have not only invested millions of dollars and worked tirelessly to drum up further financial support for the school, they have personally invested countless hours in helping to run it. The goal of the school is to give these students the same kind of educational experience and academic curriculum usually available only to children of wealthy families who send their kids to the most prestigious of private schools.

David Robinson is a living billboard for showing the difference between right and wrong. He does what he does out of the goodness of his heart.

There is something else about Robinson that puts him a cut above most other athletes of his stature. He not only makes time for the media, he seems to relish it. Soon after leaving the Navy to join the Spurs—after graduating from Annapolis and getting his commission, he served two years as a naval officer before joining the Spurs for the 1989–90 season as a twenty-four-year-old rookie—I got my first chance to interview him.

The first time I approached Robinson and asked him if he would consent to an interview, a live one at that, he quickly agreed and gave me a terrific two minutes of on-air time. So refreshing, considering the fact that I've been rejected by lesser-known athletes for requests involving much less. Robinson not only gave me the time, he made it seem as if he was as interested in doing the interview as I was in having him do it.

For a number of years, I have emceed the Philanthropy World Hall of Fame ceremony at the Fairmont Hotel in Dallas. They fly in people from all over the world, and the time it was David's turn to be inducted into the Hall of Fame, he did much more than just show up, put on a happy face, and press the flesh with anyone who could manage to get within three feet of him.

The whole time he was there, Robinson was fully engaged and gracious. He went out of his way to not only meet everyone he could, but to speak to them, and to be engaging in doing so. Everything I put in front of him for him to sign—a number of golf-related items to be given out at my golf tournament—he patiently autographed with care. I honestly believe if I had put another dozen things in front of him, he would have signed every single one of them.

A lot of time at banquets like this, the big-name folks blow into town, do their thing, and make up any excuse they can for needing to get out of there as soon as possible. And many of those have their own chartered planes standing by at the airport, ready to whisk them back home or to whatever their next destination might be. Robinson was not that way at all. In fact, he hadn't flown up from San Antonio in his own plane; he had flown commercial and booked himself the latest flight out that night, so he would have as much time as possible to spend at the banquet.

As much as my dad spoke to me about role models while I was growing up, they were usually sports figures quite a bit older than me. That's the way I always assumed it would be. Lou Gehrig, Jesse Owens, John Wooden; I had no problem looking up to them because they were, to me, adult figures who are to be respected.

As the years have gone by, new and admirable people have entered my life, giving me a whole new respect for new generations of role models who can have a positive influence on me and, in turn, my own children. I can admire and respect David Robinson even though he is quite a bit younger than I, and not just because of my love of sports. I can look up to him, not because he's seven feet, one inch tall, but because he is a man of conviction who genuinely seems to care as much for other people—even strangers— as he does for himself. Indeed, a true inspiration to all.

VII

NOLAN RYAN

DESIRE

*The difference between success and failure
can only be measured by one's desire.*

—Author unknown

You've heard the legendary pop-soul singer James Brown referred to as "the hardest-working man in show biz." You'll get no argument there. Turn the subject to baseball, though, and Nolan Ryan gets a spot among the ten or so hardest workers in baseball over the last, say, forty years.

You don't pitch for twenty-seven seasons at the major-league level, up to the ripe, old age of forty-six, without producing buckets of workout sweat between starts and during the off-season keeping yourself in shape. Ryan never met a workout he didn't pursue with gusto. Case in point: on the night he threw his seventh career no-hitter, striking out sixteen Toronto Blue Jays on May 1, 1991, Ryan patiently explained his way through the post-game media ambush and then knocked out a good workout on the stationary bike, probably mumbling the whole time what all the fuss was about.

There are precious few words to describe what it was that must have made Ryan a diamond cut above the rest. Desire comes to mind. Where millions of young boys and girls desire to have competitive fun playing sports of their choosing, it takes a hardcore desire to get to where Ryan did in baseball. He nurtured a work ethic that spurred him year after year to persevere through the muscle-straining endeavors of off-season workouts. This was so he could be primed and fit the following spring to tackle yet another grind of a baseball season that could stretch to upwards of seven months (not counting spring training). The goal was to stay sharp, focused, and ready to take the ball and take the mound every fifth day to throw more than a hundred pitches a game, each requiring the focus of a brain surgeon and the analytical skill of Sherlock Holmes trying to unlock the mystery of getting the next guy out.

Face it, you've got to really want it to achieve what Ryan did over and over again.

One of the things you have to reconcile about Ryan is his real-life persona with his on-field persona. The personalities seem diametrically opposed to one another. As polite and accommodating as he is, Ryan has never been known as the talkative sort who expound on the physics of the game or take great joy in spinning stories or regaling the room with jokes. Turn on the cassette recorder, ask a simple question, and then let him roll, right? Hardly. That's not his style. He's *sooooooo* laid back. Everything about Ryan is farm-boy Texan, a reserved conversationalist with a south-Texas drawl who speaks a simple layman's language, almost lazily. He does it with the aw-shucks manner of a guy more comfortable ambling his way across the ranch to climb up on the tractor than he is standing on a curb in the Big Apple trying to hail a cab to take him back to some glitzy hotel.

The contradiction was Ryan on the mound, all six feet two and 205 pounds of him, broad at the shoulders and thickly muscled through the legs, glaring at a batter, about to launch into a delivery that would end with him thrusting off the rubber with a powerful leg drive, as he'd deliver a pitch that would explode out of his hand and strike fear in batters as it raced toward home, topping out at over a hundred miles an hour.

Ryan talks a slow, almost nonchalant game, but out on the pitcher's mound, everything about him was fast, forceful, and straight to the point, oftentimes with the pitch bearing down right through the batter's wheel-house and the poor hitter trying to get wood on the ball while simultaneously fighting a subconscious urge to either duck or at least turn his back so he won't get killed if it hits him.

By the time Ryan retired in 1993 with 324 career victories, a record 5,714 strikeouts, and those seven no-no's, he had pitched more than 60 percent of my lifetime. More than any other sports figure, Ryan's career had truly bridged my lifetime, from my days in high school to the cusp of middle age.

When I was still in high school, Ryan was a young pitcher who had just been called up to the New York Mets, getting raves for his once-every-generation fastball, all the while stuck with a label questioning whether he would ever be able to harness that speed with enough control to stick in the majors. Before he would call it quits, I had attended college, married Carole, twice become a father, worked twenty years as a sports broadcaster (eventually landing in DFW, where I would come to know Nolan and his family), and sent my son, Doug, off to college.

If and when Nolan reads this, he's going to feel old when he sees his career placed on a timeline like this. He shouldn't feel too bad—I'm just three years behind him and hot on his trail.

Ryan's baseball career was so long that it's practically the equivalent of three-plus careers in one. After spending over three seasons with the Mets, Ryan went to the California Angels in 1972, the result of a trade that included sending Jim Fregosi to the Mets. Ryan spent eight years there—a minicareer—playing for one of his idols, Angels-owner Gene Autry (the "Singing Cowboy," no less, which must have pleased Ryan). In that time, Ryan won 138 games and teamed with Frank Tanana to forge one of that decade's best one-two pitching punches.

Ryan's first three seasons with the Halos were remarkable, considering he was essentially playing for a .500 team (as would be the case for almost his entire career). In 1972, he won nineteen games, posted a 2.28 ERA, and threw nine shutouts among his twenty complete games. He led the American League with 329 strikeouts and set a single-season record for fewest hits allowed per nine innings (5.26). In 1973, he won twenty-one games, tossed two no-hitters, pitched twenty-six complete games, and set a major-league record with 383 strikeouts. Then in 1974, he notched his third consecutive 300-strikeout season (367) and, three times, struck out nineteen batters in a game, capping his year on the last day of the season with his third career no-hitter, striking out fifteen while beating the Minnesota Twins.

By the time Ryan left the Angels after the 1979 season to pitch for the Houston Astros, he was thirty-two years old. Cynics were counting the days to when Ryan would finally blow out his arm. Doubting Thomases in those days believed that an almost purely fastball pitcher with that kind of bullet-train velocity was a sure bet to suddenly hit "the wall" and crater, that he was an early exit from the majors waiting to happen. But there were things about Ryan and the kinesiology of pitching that the baseball "experts" didn't grasp back then: 1) that much of Ryan's velocity came from his powerful leg drive, and he had always been a workout fanatic when it came to strengthening and conditioning his legs—his arm, itself, didn't have to work any harder than necessary through all those pitches; and 2) as we all know now, there is worse arm stress than throwing mostly fastballs, such as that which comes from throwing breaking pitches such as sliders and curveballs, which require various twisting and snapping motions that are not natural to throwing.

Ryan was well into his thirties before he started relying on those types of pitches as much as his peers had been doing for years. As long as he could spot his fastball and keep it in the mid-90s and higher, Ryan was almost unhittable. In his second nine-year minicareer, back in the National League, this time with the Houston Astros, Ryan won 106 games, threw his fifth no-hitter, and twice each led the league in strikeouts and ERA.

By the time Ryan got to the Texas Rangers in 1989, after a contract dispute with the Astros, he was on the high side of forty, having long since proved to the critics that a pitcher of his velocity could indeed endure a long career. He would end up pitching five seasons for the Rangers, and it was much more than a farewell tour. During his time with the Rangers, Ryan reached the coveted three-hundred-victory plateau, blew past the five-thousand-strikeout barrier, and notched his sixth and seventh career no-hitters. No other pitcher has ever had more than four.

If there's any other pitcher I can compare to Ryan, both in style and in workout ethic, the almost-obvious choice is Roger Clemens. Like Ryan, Clemens, about fifteen years younger than the Ryan Express, hails from a town not far from Houston, has stretched his career beyond twenty years with a killer workout regimen, and long has been a predominantly power pitcher who can rack up a lot of Ks in a hurry.

Ryan is so well grounded that his feet are nailed to the ground. His demeanor is watch repairman–like—calm and steady—although it is clear that there is a fire that burned inside him when he was between the chalk, focusing on the hitter like nothing else in the world counted. His desire had no peer. For someone who threw that hard more than a hundred times a game, you knew there had to be some kind of a dynamo churning inside of him. It bubbled to public display one August day in 1993, when he hit the Chicago White Sox's Robin Ventura with a slow curveball. Ventura, twenty years Ryan's junior, charged the mound, where he suddenly found himself stuck in a powerful Ryan headlock while the granddaddy-aged pitcher pummeled Ventura with one punch after another. Ventura was ejected from the game, and Ryan was allowed to continue, although his career would be over about a month and a half later when he tore a tendon in his pitching arm with two starts left to go in the 1993 season.

One other thing about Ryan I admire is that he never said no when I asked him for an interview. Never. Can you imagine Barry Bonds never saying no to a media request? And I've never seen him tout his celebrity for anything other than a TV commercial. Carole and I have attended a number of events with Ruth and Nolan over the years. We've come to know their children. Theirs is a special family. Their priorities are intact. Nolan is the all-American, family athlete with the all-American family.

There was the time after he had retired that Nolan and his wife Ruth bought a little hotel between Houston and his hometown of Alvin. While out in his pickup truck running an errand to the hotel to deliver some buckets and mops, Ryan stopped off to grab a bite at a small restaurant. The waitress told him how much he resembled Nolan Ryan, although she had no clue it was really him. When she asked him what he did, he said he was "a rancher." And he wasn't lying.

At that point, the waitress mentioned to Ryan that she had a grandson who had told her that Nolan Ryan had bought a nearby hotel and to always keep an eye out for him in case he stopped by the restaurant so that she could get his autograph for him. Soon after she had told Ryan this story, her boss, the restaurant manager, arrived and sat down with Ryan. She then said to her boss, "Doesn't that guy look like Nolan Ryan?" at which point she pulled out of her apron a Ryan baseball card her grandson had given her, just in case, to have him sign.

As Ryan stood up to leave, he asked the waitress if he could see the card again and then asked her if she wanted him to sign it, at which she said, "No, I want to save it for the real Nolan Ryan." Well, Ryan finally told her he was indeed Nolan Ryan, and when her boss vouched for it, she handed him the card, flabbergasted.

That's Nolan Ryan for you—never one to push his Hall of Fame celebrity on anybody.

VIII

GALE SAYERS

PURPOSE

The purpose of life is a life of purpose.

—Robert Byrne

T he most exciting football player I ever saw was Gale Sayers. He was to football what Sandy Koufax was to baseball and Bobby Orr to hockey—a superlative talent whose athletic career was cut short for medical reasons. For Koufax, it was the arthritic elbow in his pitching arm; for Orr and Sayers, it was devastating knee injuries that effectively ended their careers before either turned thirty. Koufax was a bit more fortunate; he was all of thirty when he retired from baseball after the 1966 season.

Every generation has its share of athletes across the sporting spectrum who not only transcend their sports but perform in such a way that when you see film of them decades later, their skills and moves never lose their freshness. Pete Maravich was one such athlete, a basketball player who came out of college in the early 1970s with the kind of eye-catching moves with the ball that look as innovative today as they did over thirty-five years ago. Sayers is another such athlete, a man with otherworldly, shifty moves that seemed to defy physics, at times his upper body going in one direction while his lower body went another.

Sayers became who and what he was by having a laser-aimed purpose in his life. Football was more than just a game to him; it was an enterprise, a mission. The yards he gained running, returning, and receiving the ball were not a random result of being the best when it came to finding the slightest cracks of daylight near the line of scrimmage or dodging would-be tacklers with some sort of innate radar system. While Sayers obviously was loaded with God-given talent, the kind that defied physics time and again, he saw football as a greater good, not just an athletic endeavor of big, sweaty bodies crashing, but as an expression of man's creativity and insight.

While football was a game to him, it also was much more. Certainly more than a job too—more like a calling, what some might call a lifework. It's a matter of choice how we go about defining what we do in life, and the more we grasp it as such, the more purpose it brings to our lives. It becomes the pursuit of our passion, characterized by the passion of how we pursue it. That was Gale Sayers and football.

When I picture Gale Sayers, I envision a time where there seemed to be more black-and-white sets than color, long before there were super slo-mo, reverse-angle replays, and all those other network special effects that jazz up a sporting telecast. What we got with Sayers was jaw-dropping moves, speed, quickness, and guile in real time; at times his upper torso seemingly unhinged from his hips, or his arms went in one direction and his legs in another. The great players down through the years provided human-highlight reels; Sayers was the human optical illusion, his lightning-quick spikes chewing up and spitting out tufts of muddy turf as he made another one of his contortional cuts. If Sayers had ever bothered to register every different kind of move he ever made on a football field, he would have owned more patents than Edison and Gates combined.

Sayers not only had great speed and body control, he had an innate ability to find holes or "see" would-be tacklers before they came into view, avoiding trouble by either twisting or otherwise contorting his body in such a way so as to elude danger. Just as Nolan Ryan threatened to throw a no-hitter every time he took the mound, Sayers threatened to score a touchdown any time he touched the ball. In one unforgettable game on a cold, gray, muddy December day in 1965, Sayers practically did just that.

As a rookie halfback for the Chicago Bears, Sayers tied a National Football League record that day by scoring six touchdowns against the San Francisco 49ers. Sayers, a six-foot, two-hundred pounder out of the University of Kansas, scored on an 80-yard screen pass, an 85-yard punt return, and on runs of 21, 7, 50, and 1 yards. All told, he accounted for 336 yards—113 rushing, 89 receiving, and 134 returning punts.

Sayers ended his rookie season of 1965 with an NFL rookie record twenty-two touchdowns, and he was named league rookie of the year. It turned out that while 1965 was Sayers's first year in the NFL, it would be the last season for the undisputed king among league running backs, the incomparable Jim Brown of the Cleveland Browns. Brown was only thirty when he retired as the game's career rushing leader to pursue a career in Hollywood. In leaving the game, Brown was in effect handing off the baton of premier NFL back to his obvious successor, Sayers.

There was so much about Sayers and his elusive running style, complete with the ability to change direction on a dime or burst through a tiny hole with unmatched acceleration, that made him special. Pulitzer Prize-winning sportswriter Red Smith once wrote the following:

> "His days at the top of his game were numbered, but there was magic about him that still sets him apart from the other great running backs in pro football. He wasn't a bruiser like Jimmy Brown, but he could slice through the middle like a warm knife through butter, and when he took a pitchout and peeled around the corner, he was the most exciting thing in pro football."

Sayers followed up his sensational rookie season by winning the NFL rushing title in 1966, gaining what would be a career-high 1,231 yards (in a fourteen-game season). It would be the first of two rushing titles for him, the second coming in 1969, when he gained 1,032 yards a year after missing half of the previous season due to the injury he received when hit by the 49ers' Kermit Alexander. Sayers suffered ruptured cartilage and two torn ligaments in his right knee. After his sterling 1969 comeback, Sayers was awarded the George Halas Award, symbolic of his being "the most courageous player in professional football."

If Sayers had had a vote for the award, though, he might have put in for one of his former teammates. At the awards ceremony, Sayers dedicated it to friend and teammate Brian Piccolo, a fellow running back and halfback rival of Sayers's who was dying of cancer. The story of the rivalry-turned-friendship between Piccolo and Sayers would be made into a memorable 1971 made-for-TV tearjerker, *Brian's Song*, starring Billy Dee Williams (of later *Star Wars* fame as Lando Calrissian) as Sayers and James Caan (Sonny Corleone in *The Godfather*) as Piccolo.

In a 1970 exhibition game, Sayers suffered ligament damage in his left knee, and his playing days were numbered. He would play two regular-season games before going under the knife, and he would never regain the trademark elusiveness and quickness. He ended up retiring in 1971 after playing only two games that season. In seven injury-interrupted seasons, Sayers would play a total of only sixty-eight games, finishing with just under five thousand career yards while never even reaching the one thousand mark in career carries. He scored fifty-six touchdowns, eight of which came on kickoff or punt returns.

Sayers was one of a select few athletes I idolized while growing up in the '60s, so it tickled me to no end when I got to meet him long after he had retired, first to work in the athletic department at his alma mater, Kansas, and later to become athletic director at Southern Illinois. Then in 1984, Sayers left athletic administration to start Chicago-based Crest Computer Supply Company, which provides hardware and service for Fortune 500 companies. Ten years after its inception, Crest posted more than $55 million in sales. That, too, is the product of realized purpose. It's Sayers.

Sayers is one of the most soft-spoken people I've ever met, someone to whom you practically have to cock an ear to hear him when he speaks. When he played, you didn't have to hear him to know that he's special. And he's never changed. In many ways, his dignified demeanor reminds me a great deal of tennis Hall of Famer Arthur Ashe, baseball immortal Jackie Robinson, and Oscar-winning actor Sidney Poitier—all four incredible talents and inspiring individuals with paramount purpose in their lives. Sayers's football-playing career was incomplete, but it was spectacular, and his off-field success since is a testament to what a great role model he was, and is.

IX

HOWARD COSELL

CANDOR

There is no wisdom like frankness.

—Benjamin Disraeli

H oward Cosell was bigger than life. If you didn't know that, he would have been happy to tell you. The most time I ever spent with the bombastic television sportscaster was about thirty minutes, which started with a shared elevator ride up to a football press box one time for *Monday Night Football*. We had a good talk and discussed a number of topics, from football to fighting, including the infamous "no mas" debacle at the Superdome in November 1981 between Sugar Ray Leonard and Roberto Duran, which we were both ringside for. But what struck me most about him was how serious he was about things. I also felt a touch of arrogance, which I presume he knew was part of public perception, and he made no effort to hide it.

It says a lot about Cosell that at the height of his career, which arguably was the years he spent on *MNF* (1970–83), a national poll pegged him as the least favorite sportscaster in America. The same poll showed him to be the most popular sportscaster in America. No shock there—with Howard Cosell, just like it was with my dad, it was all about black and white with little room for shades of gray.

As he often proclaimed, Cosell told it like it was. Like it or not. He was blunt; he was conceited; he was politically incorrect. With nasal voice and all, he was as much solely responsible for revolutionizing sports broadcasting, actually sports journalism as a whole, as Woodward and Bernstein were for taking investigative journalism to a new plateau. Cosell never backed down from an interview and was never afraid to ask the tough questions, even the ones that could have gotten him punched in the nose on any stage other than ABC Sports.

Cosell was one of those rare network-TV sportscasters who could rightfully say with a straight face that he was a "journalist," and no one would laugh.

Cosell helped revolutionize how television covered sports, taking it from the bland and understated to the sublime and controversial. He personified the quasi-renegade personality that ABC Sports brought to the table, thanks to the innovative handiwork of Roone Arledge, especially during the 1960s and 1970s. Next to the understated tone and muted visuals of seasoned veterans CBS and NBC, ABC was loud, with its bright-yellow blazers and its luscious visuals and audacious audio, with an assortment of camera angles and mike placements never before seen in network sports. ABC was FOX before there was FOX.

In its deviceful heyday, ABC Sports was the new kid on the block, the proverbial upstart trying out a new bag of tricks that included more announcers in the booth and on the sidelines, or in pit row (e.g., Chris Economaki with handheld mike yelling above the din of roaring cars speeding by at two hundred miles an hour while he reported from trackside.) It was Jim McKay taking ABC's growing legions on a trip around the world every weekend; it was Dandy Don, Handsome Frank, and Shrill, Hyperbolic Howard Cosell eventually settling into one booth, barely coexisting in a civil manner while making pro football a prime-time spectacle.

It was HOW-wudd COE-selllll, SPEAK-ing of SPORTS (emphasizing the nasal pop on his Ps)!

Cosell, who passed away in 1995 at the age of seventy-seven, is most renowned for two things: his love-hate relationship with boxer Muhammad Ali that turned into an impromptu act of sorts with each being an on-air foil for the other, and his fourteen-year stint with *MNF*. He could speak with ample depth on a variety of topics, so, yeah, it's fair to say he was a smart guy. Talking to him was almost like talking to a college professor. The longer I spoke with him, though, the more relaxed he got, and I even got the sense that he was starting to forget who he was supposed to be.

Considering his candor, boldness, and command of the English language, Cosell could have passed himself off as an attorney. In fact, he was. After graduating Phi Beta Kappa from Columbia University, he went on to New York University Law School. He would go on to practice law in New York for eight years before making a dramatic career change in 1954. Cosell strapped a large tape recorder to his back and took a job interviewing baseball players, making a name for himself with his brusque, confrontational manner. Broadcast journalism would never be the same.

Occasionally, I am asked what I thought of Cosell and whether his style had any influence on my own sportscasting career. Nothing on the surface. Certainly, my personality and on-air delivery were 180 degrees from where he was. Cosell was rarely conventional and conforming, but often controversial and confrontational. As for speech patterns, Cosell spoke slowly, enunciating his words with careful emphasis, where I tend to speak at a clip that's much more upbeat and conversational. Then again, his commitment to broadcast journalism, which involves reporting as much as announcing, did influence me.

The one night everything collided for me was a Thursday night in February 1989, when on the 10:00 p.m. newscast we broke the story that Bum Bright was selling the Dallas Cowboys to Jerry Jones. It had already been reported earlier in the day by another media outlet that the Cowboys were probably going to be sold to L.A. Lakers owner Jerry Buss. But we had a reliable source very close to the negotiations—we had been staying in touch for weeks on this—who had told us it was going to be Jones, not Buss. I knew the information we had was correct, but my boss, the news director, wanted me to go with Buss in my report or tell him who our source was so he could attempt to confirm it. I told him I couldn't compromise the trust our source had in us, so I could not share that information with him. That didn't make him happy.

But I knew for certain Jerry Jones was the buyer. Our source was that knowledgeable. So if I was going to "tell it like it is," I was going to stick to the story I knew was correct, not a speculated report heard on some other media outlet. At some point that night, it did cross my mind that I might be putting my job in jeopardy and could end up getting fired, but I felt confident and comfortable with all we had. I can remember calling both Carole and my agent to get them prepared for the worst-case scenario. My agent told me not to worry, assuring me nothing was going to happen.

With this being must-see-TV night on NBC, my boss wanted to promote the 10:00 p.m. newscast with a teaser about our story, and I told him I thought we should hold off. I didn't want another media outlet such as Associated Press or a TV competitor hearing the promos and then going out and quickly trying to get the story before we even actually reported it, even though at the last minute that likely wasn't going to happen. The other part of the scenario was that I had known both Tex Schramm (Cowboys general manager) and Tom Landry (head coach) for many years, and I didn't want them hearing this story for the first time on our newscast without some sort of warning. I needed to get in touch with them before we publicly aired the story, simply as a courtesy to them.

About five or ten minutes before I went on the air at 10:00 pm, I tried to phone Coach Landry to tell him what I was reporting, but there was no answer at his home. I hung up and redialed on the chance that I had dialed a wrong number, but this time I got a busy signal. I then called Tex. I told him I was sorry, but that I had some bad news concerning the Cowboys, inform- ing Tex that Arkansas businessman Jerry Jones was going to buy the team and assume the duties of president and general manager. In addition, Jimmy Johnson would take over as head coach, leaving Landry, like Schramm, with- out the jobs they had proudly held for twenty nine years. That was easily the worst part of the night. Having to inform Schramm and Landry that the end had come, abrupt as it might have been.

After a few seconds of silence, Tex said I had it wrong, and the reason he "knew" I had it wrong was because he had been asked by Bright to sell the team. But what Tex didn't know was that Bright had given the research firm of Solomon Brothers the go-ahead to complete the sale to Jones. Tex had no idea, and when I asked him for a comment that I could use on the air, all he said to me was, "Scott, that's news to me." He was totally in the dark.

By then, I was out of time. I had to get into the studio for our broadcast, so I asked Tex if he would please call Coach Landry on my behalf and tell him that this was the story we were reporting. We had the story first, but I also wanted to make sure we reported it with dignity and humanity.

It was a wild night all around, and right after I went off the air, I phoned Jerry Jones at The Mansion, where he was staying. He immediately told me that he had been watching and confirmed that we had the story correct on all accounts, adding that he had definitely reached an agreement with Bright to buy the Cowboys.

When I recall that night, it's easy to think of journalists like Howard Cosell and what he might have done had he been in my shoes—in other words, the whole "telling it like it is" thing. On that night, at least, I think we all passed the Cosell litmus test. We had the story, and we were sticking to it. And as it turned out, we were right on all accounts. Obviously, that brought about a collective sigh of relief.

Stories like this are what you get into this business for in the first place—to be a part of big, breaking, investigative news stories, digging as deep as you can possibly dig, checking and re-checking your sources, making certain you have all of the facts correct, all the time working against the clock so you can beat the competition and be first with the story you're working on for your viewers. We had worked for months on this story. I'm proud to this day of the great team effort from all the guys in our little sports department at NBC 5 that didn't even number half a dozen. Television stations traditionally lack the staff to break a story of this magnitude. But we did it, and the experience was certainly fun and incredibly rewarding. There is no question; breaking the story on the sale of America's Team was easily the biggest investigative story I was ever a part of.

X

ROGER STAUBACH

LEADERSHIP

The ultimate measure of a man is not where he stands in moments of comfort and convenience, but where he stands at times of challenge and controversy.

—Martin Luther King Jr.

Over the years I have come to know Roger Staubach probably as well as any other DFW sports figure I have come in contact with over the past twenty-five years. Which is pretty telling, considering that by the time I had arrived to work in the DFW market, Staubach already had retired from pro football.

Obviously, this guy is no recluse.

Ironically, I started out hating Staubach and the Dallas Cowboys, and that's because I grew up a New York Giants fan. To love the Giants in the late '60s and into the '70s meant to despise the Cowboys and to get exasperated with Staubach because he was always leading the 'Boys to some sort of victory, comeback, or some other means over the Giants.

The fact that I felt that way about Staubach was proof that, deep down, I really admired him for what he was able to accomplish as a quarterback. He was one of the best fourth-quarter quarterbacks the game has ever known. If one player from an opposing team can get me that riled up, it tells me that he's doing something pretty special, at least when you look at it from the Cowboys' standpoint.

Of all the words that can be used to accurately describe Staubach and his worthiness as a role model, "leadership" and "composure" define him best. Leading the way while staying cool under pressure. Taking his game up a notch in the crunch times when others around him were losing their focus, their confidence, or their lunch. When his team was down and there were less than two minutes to play, Staubach was a rock, an almost-sure bet not to fumble, not to throw the ball in the wrong place, not to call the wrong play, not to make a bad decision at the wrong time.

It's like this: they say in golf that when it gets late in the final round and flop sweat is forming on palms and backswings are getting shorter and quicker, the great ones actually slow down, and when they get to the green they see a hole that gets bigger all the time. In football, and for clutch performers such as Staubach, what they see as time running out and the end drawing near is a game clock that seems to slow down for them. Plays unfold in front of them as if in slow motion, and suddenly their senses are more acute and their responses better measured.

One irony is that for as many years as I did TV sports in the DFW area—over twenty years—and considering how Staubach was still such a prominent icon all those years, I never saw him play from the perspective of a DFW sportscaster. Staubach had retired at the relatively young age of thirty-seven—one story is that doctors had advised him to do so because of numerous concussions—in 1979, about a year before I moved from Washington, D.C. to DFW.

I did get to cover Cowboys games and interview Staubach twice a year with the Redskins and Cowboys playing each other at home and away as NFC East rivals. I also got to see some other Cowboys games over those years as a pool reporter for a group of TV stations in Washington, New York, Los Angeles, Chicago, and Cleveland that were all owned and operated by NBC. As neat as it was finally getting to interview Staubach after rooting against him and the Cowboys, it was an even bigger kick for my dad.

From the time Staubach was at the Naval Academy in the early 1960s, winning the Heisman in 1963, Dad would rave about Staubach, bragging about what a great leader he was. Dad always loved the service academies because they embodied the very values he was trying to instill in me, and I reckon Dad would have been thrilled had I gone to West Point or Annapolis or Colorado Springs, even if not to play football.

To this day, it pleases me to no end when I bump into Roger at an event like the annual Military Ball in Dallas because it's like I'm seeing one of

Dad's favorite poster boys for all that is right about the world. Roger doesn't know this, and he might squirm to read it, but seeing him is like getting a greeting card from Dad. And I'm all right with that.

The thing about leaders, the really good ones, is that they not only get others to look up to them; they also elevate everyone else's game. People can lead in so many ways: by example, by their inspiring words, by what they stand for. They engender trust, and they stand alone. They are an inspiration to those around them, always functioning with great composure. The best ones are so good at what they do, they put more fans in the seats, and that's why they get paid more. In that regard, Dad always would point out Sandy Koufax. Staubach also was in that group.

Not only was Staubach the ultimate leader on the football field, having a hand in getting the Cowboys to five Super Bowls—winning two of them—and emerging as the master of the two-minute drill and the author of the Hail Mary Pass, but he also asserted himself as a highly successful leader off the field. Just look at the Staubach Company, dealing in commercial real estate and company relocation—they've got offices all over the country and around the world. He's one guy who would be welcome in *any* board room in America.

The Hall of Fame quarterback honors his commitments as a man of his word, even when he doesn't feel up to it. Literally. One year when I was emceeing the Military Ball in Dallas, Staubach showed up as promised for the Friday night pre-event and made the rounds, even though he was sick as a dog. He was supposed to come back on Saturday, but a 105-degree fever confined him to bed, although his wife Marianne gamely showed up in his place at the official ball.

Competitive fire? Roger is not one to brag, but he doesn't mind telling stories that demonstrate he still has a knack for winning, to include contests other than his beloved pickup basketball games. One of his favorite stories is from the recent Super Bowl, for which he was asked to play quarterback in an all-star game involving retired, former–Super Bowl players, most of whom were in their late thirties or forties. The opposing quarterback was someone much younger than Roger; it might have been either Jim Kelly or Dan Marino.

When Roger walked into the locker room and his teammates saw him, they just kind of shook their heads and started laughing. After all, here's Roger, now in his sixties, about to lead a bunch of guys half his age. No one was laughing after the game in which Roger, still in great shape, passed for a bunch of touchdowns and was named the MVP.

It was just like in the old days, when Staubach and company were beating up on my Giants. Some things never change, and thankfully, when it comes to leadership, Staubach falls into that category.

WALTER PAYTON

SACRIFICE

*He who would accomplish little must
sacrifice little; he who would achieve much
must sacrifice much; but he who would
attain highly must sacrifice greatly.*

—James Allen

If you want to start a great debate about football, ask a group of fans who the greatest running back in National Football League history was. There are as many valid answers as there are days in the week. It just depends on what your criteria and your preferred style of running back are.

If you like the big, power-back type of player, someone who combines strength with guile, the obvious pick is Jim Brown. In a pinch, Eric Dickerson will do. If you're more into speed and elusiveness, someone who can slash, dart, and contort his body to elude would-be tacklers, you might go for Gale Sayers or O.J. Simpson. The latter was a superb running back long before he was a mediocre TV-booth commentator or world-renowned murder suspect.

Then there are the smaller guys, shorter and yet muscular, who are a step or two shy of world-class speed but are masters at following blockers, slithering through fast-closing holes or bumping it outside and taking it down the side for the long haul, stiff-arming or shoulder-banging their way to extra yards. Tony Dorsett. Emmitt Smith. Barry Sanders. Each a little bit different from the other, but all in a class of great runners good to have around.

Then there is Walter Payton, who brought joy to his game, pain to defenders who tried to tackle him straight up, and durability to the playing field. "Sweetness" missed only one game in his thirteen seasons as a Chicago Bear, often playing with injuries running the gamut from minor to borderline debilitating. Yet he never spoke about the persistent aches that would have slowed, or more likely benched, other players. Payton was a terrific blocking back and a pass-receiving threat out of the backfield, yet most of all he was a great running back after taking the handoff.

Payton was the consummate pro when it came to servant-leadership; he was willing to sacrifice his own comfort, his own body, to give to the team, to keep on ticking like some sort of human Energizer Bunny who kept on playing, missing only that one game in his entire career. This is how Payton led—by example, throwing his body at opponents—all in a selfless way to give his team a better chance of winning week to week.

Opposing defensive players, long after No. 34 had retired, said this about Payton: when it came to the fourth quarter of even the most hard-fought games, Payton was the freshest player on the field in the third and fourth quarters. By then, defensive players were weary from having to try and stop the contact-loving Payton. When Payton had the ball, he went out of his way to drive himself into tacklers. Payton's philosophy was that when he was about to get hit, he would drive a shoulder, knee, head, or elbow into his adversary, his law-of-physics reasoning being that the collision would in effect buffer the impact on his own body while knocking the tackler down a peg for the remainder of the game.

When asked once what his advice would be for opposing defenses intent on stopping him, Payton said, "The night before the game, I guess they'd have to kidnap me."

More than likely, Payton gave a hearty laugh after answering the question because that was part of his nature as "Sweetness." Payton loved to laugh and joke around, even while taking the game so seriously. He just didn't take himself seriously. Over the years, the most enduring Bears players have been the ones with a great sense of humor. "Da Bears" have had more break-even or losing seasons than anyone in the Windy City cares to remember, as was the case for much of the first nine seasons of Payton's career.

Payton was Everyman, someone who happened to have God-given talent and drive that most mortals can only dream about. Chicago-area citizens never knew when they might run into Payton; he was that accessible and out and about. It could be at a mall, a gas station, or a restaurant. Approach him for an autograph, and you would not only get his signature but more than likely a conversation as well. If you wanted to touch a part of his life, all he asked for was the chance to know your name in return. As they say, he was that kind of guy.

Although rich, Payton did not keep himself and family in seclusion. Many Chicago residents knew exactly where he lived, and it wasn't behind security fences and guard shacks. One summerlike day when Payton was washing his car out in his driveway, some fans drove by, slowing down to see his house as though they were on a Hollywood tour of movie stars' homes. But they were in for a surprise. When Payton saw them slow down, he lowered his hose—certainly fighting off the temptation to playfully spray them—and motioned for them to stop and come over. They did, and after a few minutes of genuine, friendly conversation, they were practically friends for life.

Writing about Payton would be incomplete without the facts and figures. When Payton retired after the 1987 season, he had set an NFL career rushing record with 16,726 yards, about four thousand more than previous record holder Jim Brown totaled in his comparatively brief career. His mark would stand until 2002, when Emmitt Smith, then still with the Dallas Cowboys, broke the record.

Payton's finest season numbers-wise was 1977, when he rushed for a career-high and league-leading 1,852 yards en route to winning NFL MVP honors. Even more amazing was his single-game accomplishment of November 20 that season when, two days after being bed ridden with the flu, Payton rushed for 275 yards, breaking Simpson's single-game mark by two yards. However, it wouldn't be until 1985 that Payton's career got the final stamp of approval, a Super Bowl ring featuring the greatest Bears team of all time, coached by Mike Ditka.

Payton had another stellar season in that Super Bowl year of 1985, rushing for 1,551 yards while also averaging ten yards a catch on forty-nine receptions. All that was missing from his résumé that year was a Super Bowl touchdown. Offensive lineman William "the Refrigerator" Perry—not Payton—got the late-game, short-yardage nod to score the frosting-on-the-cake touchdown for the Bears on their way to a 46–10 victory over the New England Patriots. It probably should have been Payton's moment, but Ditka opted for the gimmick Perry play.

Not only was Payton an extraordinarily tough guy, an incredibly durable player with a selfless attitude, he also had a tireless work ethic. He could often be found working out on the outskirts of the city on a levee with a forty-five-degree angle, running up and down the steep slope time after time, building his endurance and leg strength to nearly superhuman levels.

Twelve years after retiring, Payton passed away at age forty-five in 1999, the victim of bile duct cancer that was discovered while he was undergoing treatment for primary sclerosing cholangitis, a rare liver disease. Like Lou Gehrig before him, Payton died before his time, leaving behind a legacy of extraordinary achievements and humanity mixed with humility, and that's why I have long had a deep appreciation for Sweetness.

Aside from covering and interviewing Walter several times, I only spent time with him away from the field on a couple of occasions. One was the night he was a guest of the Doak Walker National Running Back Awards Presentation ceremony. My wife, Carole, was seated at the head table next to Walter during the evening, and all she could talk about later was how gracious, polite, and kind he was the whole time, a perfect gentleman. That's how I'll always remember Sweetness. No wonder the NFL named its Man of the Year award after him—annually honoring a player's volunteer and charity work as well as his excellence on the field—shortly after his death in 1999.

Dad had Lou Gehrig; I had Walter Payton.

HANK AARON

HUMILITY

Humility is like underwear, essential, but indecent if it shows.

—Helen Nielsen

As the 2006 baseball season opened, Hank Aaron was back in the consciousness of baseball fans across America. Not for anything he had done lately, but for his landmark role in baseball's record book, with his long-standing mark of 755 career home runs, a record supposedly about to be assaulted by one Barry Bonds. The names Bonds and Aaron more and more were making their way into sentences together.

Bonds began the 2006 season with 708 career home runs but with a dark cloud hanging over his head. Rampant rumors about Bonds's alleged use of performance-enhancing drugs, fueled in large part by a Bonds-damning book coming out at the same time, raised an ethical quandary: If Bonds were to indeed catch and then surpass Aaron's career home-run mark, should he get an asterisk-less spot in the record book or be deemed unjust and therefore left out?

If nothing else, the swirl of debate surrounding Bonds and his allegedly tainted career has done one good thing: it has brought Hank Aaron back into our American consciousness. And no one could be more deserving. For the right reasons at that. It's a pretty safe bet that Aaron never used steroids or any other form of performance-enhancing drugs, yet he surpassed Babe Ruth's previous record 714 home runs and didn't stop until he got to 755, and he did all that without benefit of one single season of fifty or more home runs. In those days, the Aaron Era stretching from the early 1950s to the mid-1970s, neither he nor the ball (as far as we know) was juiced, making his 755 homers that much more impressive.

I'm sure thousands of people to this day will claim that they were there the night of April 8, 1974, when Aaron made baseball history by hitting his

715th homer to pass Ruth as baseball's home run king. Actually, there were 53,775 in attendance, then an Atlanta's Fulton County Stadium record for a game, although millions more watched on TV.

I actually was one of those 53,000-plus, I'm proud to say. It was an electric kind of night, a nonstop buzz in the air on an early spring evening, fans out in full force to be a part of history (at least hopefully, as there was no guarantee that Aaron would hit the record-breaking homer in the game, or the next—think Barry Bonds back when he was chasing No. 714). Yes, it was a school night, but I could look around me and see school-aged fans everywhere, out to bask in what would turn out to be a sleepless night for all of us—sleepless in the good sense.

Most of us had a drink, hotdog, and/or bag of popcorn in our hands, but it's not like anyone was guzzling down their Coke or beer or slamming down the edibles. We were too caught up in the moment to fully engorge, or should I say engage, in the consumption of our concessions, preferring instead to share nervous chatter with one another. Besides, no one wanted to be caught with too much stuff in our hands, lest we blow a chance to catch the historic ball once (and if) Aaron launched it.

I was seated in the left-field stands about five rows behind a fellow who had brought the huge expandable net in hopes of catching the record-breaking ball. He never got the chance, and, obviously, neither did I. As baseball trivia experts know all too well, those honors went to Braves relief pitcher Tom House, who outscrambled about ten other bullpen occupants to catch Aaron's ball as it landed there, out of the reach of any fans. That remains House's biggest claim to fame, although he was a pretty good reliever for a number of years and would later become the pitching coach for the Texas Rangers under Bobby Valentine, allowing me to get to know him while I was covering the Rangers. Once again, small world.

A quick note about Tom: like me, his college major was psychology, so we shared an affinity for knowing how people think and how they respond to stimuli in their lives. Without question, House could have written the book on a thinking man's guide to baseball (at least the pitching part of it), and while with the Rangers at least, he was known for what in those days were considered quirky methods and drills for making his pitchers better. Things like having his pitchers throw footballs in practice instead of baseballs, contending that the throwing mechanics were very similar. As a sports psychologist, he was very much into the study of motion analysis, mechanical efficiency, and biomechanics. House would troubleshoot through the use of video and computer-generated, 3-D motion analysis. Among his pupils were Nolan Ryan and Randy Johnson. Whether in person, in videos, or in books, House provided the drills to improve the skills.

Tom could be a fun guy—albeit a brainy guy who knew he was looked at as kind of a geek, worn glasses and all—and who took some pride and never lived down his small role for posterity's sake in Aaron's 715th home run.

At least we know what became of House after that April night in Atlanta. I've always wondered what became of those two teenage guys who came out of the stands and ran out onto the field to congratulate Aaron as he rounded second base and headed to third on his home-run trot.

Even though I never actually covered the Braves while Aaron was active with them, I did get to know Hammerin' Hank a little bit over the years. It doesn't take an insider's knowledge to know how well grounded and authentically humble the guy was and is. I met him at some Oldtimers' games and once had him as a guest on my *Heroes and Legends* radio show. Great guy to talk to, and someone, while relatively quiet, who is quite firm in his beliefs and convictions and not shy about stating them.

Bobby Bragan, one of the most colorful characters in the history of baseball and a longtime friend, calls Aaron the greatest player he ever managed. Even today, at eighty-eight years of age, in his office daily, busy raising scholarship money for young people through his Bobby Bragan Youth Foundation, he'll tell you, "I always looked for the fun, the emotion, and the humor in the game." Like the time, when managing the struggling Braves in Milwaukee, he announced at a press conference to great cheers that he was leaving town. "That," he said, "is the good news. The bad news is I'm taking the team with me." That was the mid-1960s when the Braves moved from Milwaukee to Atlanta, making Bragan the only man to ever manage the team in both cities.

Another great bit of trivia that Bobby loves to share is the fact that Aaron really homered 756 times in his major league career, not 755 as the record states. Seems Hank was at the plate when the Cardinals pitcher, Curt Simmons, threw a ball that was just out of his normal reach. So Hammerin' Hank stepped toward the ball, took a swing, and hammered it out of the park. Aaron started his home run trot, not hearing that the home plate umpire had signaled out. As he rounded the bases and touched the plate, the ump informed him he had made contact with the ball while out of the batter's box. So he was out, and the homer did not count. Bragan argued the call on Hank's behalf so vehemently that he was tossed and watched the rest of the game from the clubhouse—but not before he saw Aaron's home run that was, and then wasn't. As for the veteran Simmons, who spent twenty years in the bigs, he was obviously impressed with the athletic ability of Aaron, as his quote, "Trying to throw a fastball by Henry Aaron is like trying to sneak a sunrise past a rooster" remains on the National Baseball Hall of Fame Web site to this day.

During Aaron's playing days from 1954 through 1976, at least for the first three-quarters of his career, even the greatest baseball players—or athletes in any pro sport, for that matter—got a fraction of the attention and airtime that sports figures do today. There was no Internet and blogging or Barry Bonds-ian Web sites back then; no ESPN, no glut of sports-talk radio. There weren't many agents either.

Ballplayers' exposure on a national level, for the most part, was limited to the occasional brief interview before an NBC *Game of the Week* or on the pages of *Sports Illustrated,* the *Sporting News,* or *Sport Magazine.* Even on a local level, the only other thing fans were privy to involving their favorite players was perhaps a post-game spot on the radio broadcast. As well as we think we know prominent athletes today, in Aaron's days they were practically reclusive, by circumstance, and on top of that Aaron lacked the flash and dash of peers such as Willie Mays and Sandy Koufax. There just wasn't room in those days for a lot of hype, and Aaron certainly wasn't the type of guy who went out of his way to seek it or to promote himself.

Aaron's relative lack of visibility is conspicuous, even by those yester-year standards. It might even have hurt him somewhat in terms of honors and due recognition. For one thing, he spent half his career in Milwaukee, certainly not a big media market, and even after the Braves moved to Atlanta in 1966, the central-Georgia city was nowhere near as big a market as it is today, thanks to the likes of Ted Turner. At least that's how I remember it. Think about it: two of Aaron's biggest "rivals" for the public consciousness were Mickey Mantle and Willie Mays. The former played his entire career in New York, which is where Mays began and much later ended his own career. Where Mays and Mantle could get photographed for getting out of a cab, Aaron could win an MVP Award (which he did at age twenty-three in 1957; incredibly, it would be his only one, earned while leading the Braves to the World Series Championship) and still get his name misspelled.

Another thing that might have held Aaron back in terms of public persona was the fact that not only did he never hit sixty home runs in a season, à la Ruth, he never even hit fifty. And in those pre-steroid days (we think), fifty home runs in a season was something special, not the roadkill it has been since the late 1990s, as pumped-up musclemen started racing past sixty-five and then seventy home runs. The most Aaron ever hit in a season was forty-seven (in 1971), although strangely, he would hit forty-four—matching his uniform number—four times. Go figure.

Still, ask any baseball fan familiar with the '50s and '60s to name the best outfielder of that era, and the top two answers almost always will remain Mantle or Mays. Okay, then. Let's narrow in a little closer: How about the best *right fielder* of that generation (both Mays and Mantle played center)? You know what? Many fans will still skip over Aaron and pick Roberto Clemente, which certainly isn't a bad pick. Clemente was a terrific player who accumulated exactly three thousand hits, could run the bases, was great with the glove, and had a gun for an arm. As much as Aaron was steady, Clemente was spectacular, even in his tragic death, the result of a plane crash while taking aid to earthquake victims in Nicaragua.

Still, the numbers, if not the star power, make a convincing case on Aaron's behalf. In addition to his 755 career homers, he ended his career as baseball's all-time leader in runs batted in (2,297), total bases (6,856), and extra-base hits (1,477), he tied Ruth for third in runs scored (2,174), and earned third (by himself) in hits (3,771). He was the first player ever to get both three thousand hits and five hundred home runs; he played in twenty-four All-Star Games; and he was the only player to hit thirty or more homers in fifteen different seasons.

Aaron accomplished all this without "the juice." Consider this: at six feet tall, the most he ever weighed as a player was 190 pounds, a number that the likes of Bonds and Sammy Sosa haven't seen since who knows when. Aaron's power came in large part from his forearms and wrists, thickly muscled from his days as a young man doing exhaustive manual labor when he wasn't playing baseball.

His feats were measured by gaudy stats, but his fortitude was measured by his endurance—physical, mental, and emotional. After hitting forty home runs in only 392 at bats in 1973—at age thirty-nine, no less—Aaron went into the 1974 season with 713 home runs, just one behind Ruth. All winter long and into the following spring he was constantly reminded of his impending breakage of Ruth's record, and many of the reminders were racist letters that were belittling and sometimes threatening. One such letter stated, "Dear Nigger Henry, You are (not) going to break this record established by the great Babe Ruth if I can help it. . . . Whites are far more superior than jungle bunnies. . . . My gun is watching your every black move."

Aaron bravely endured the taunts and threats and came back to smash Ruth's record and move on.

When I had Aaron on my radio show, he was a terrific guest, candid and yet gracious. If he harbors any bitterness, I didn't detect it.

Back in the early 1990s, my *Scott's Kids* mentoring program on television won first place in the Big Brothers Big Sisters of America Journalism Awards program, and I was flown to California to receive the award. It just so happened that the three national spokespersons for Big Brothers Big Sisters were actress Pam Dawber, retired football great Lynn Swann, and Aaron, with whom there was an instant connection as we reminisced about America's pastime back in the days when the game was a positive social force. Years later we would share the dais again at a fund-raiser in Texas for Big Brothers Big Sisters.

What goes around, comes around, and with Bonds bearing in on his record, things have sort of come full circle for Aaron as well. Aaron has made no bones about his disdain for players who have hit home runs using steroids, but he stops short of accusing any specific players, including Bonds. If there's one thing that Aaron believes in, it is the purity of the game of baseball, which is why I wouldn't hold my breath for Aaron to show up at the ballpark if and when Bonds ever gets to 754.

After retiring from the Braves, Aaron became one of the first African Americans to get into upper-level management in Major League Baseball, holding down front-office positions with the Braves, later also to get involved with Turner Broadcasting and the Airport Network.

Even if Aaron's home run record does get surpassed someday, his reputation will always be intact with me. Don't just take my word for it, either.

One time when I was interviewing another Hall of Fame player, a pitcher, and I asked him who he thought was the greatest everyday player in baseball history. He said, "All things considered, if I had to pick one, it would have to be Aaron." The source of that proclamation: none other than Nolan Ryan.

XIII

DOAK WALKER

VERSATILITY

How far you go in life depends on your being tender with the young, compassionate with the aged, sympathetic with the striving, and tolerant of the weak and strong. Because someday in your life you will have been all of these.

—George Washington Carver

Of all the sports figures featured in this book, Doak Walker might be the most obscure—if you can call him that, considering that one of the most prominent, individual college-football awards annually given out is named for Walker.

The award goes to the best running back in college football, as selected by an expert panel, and even though the award still is less than twenty years old, it has emerged as one of the most prestigious prizes in college football, just a notch or two below the Heisman Trophy and in a class of individual awards that also includes the likes of the Jim Thorpe Award, the Davey O'Brien Award, the Lombardi Award, and the Maxwell Award.

If Doak Walker isn't a household name outside Texas or Detroit, there's good reason for it. He retired from football more than fifty years ago at age twenty-eight, long before pro football had become a weekly fixture on network television. I was still a little guy, although my dad back then was a sold-out Doak Walker fan, and what was there not to like about him? He was great-looking, he had a hero's countenance, and some say that he was the greatest all-around player of his era before calling it quits with the Detroit Lions after the 1955 season.

It's well-rounded talent of Walker that made him so special in my mind, someone who could do a lot of things well and, in so doing, show himself to be a valuable member of a team despite his smaller size. Being versatile in the Walker sense doesn't mean being a super kind of man, great at whatever he touches, but someone with a willingness to do whatever it takes to contribute to the success of an organization, someone who can stretch himself or herself to ably perform tasks beyond that which is in the job description.

Doak Walker was a terrific role model because while he might not have been the best at any one thing that he did, he was a masterful multitasker.

Walker's overall spectacular play combined with his early retirement from the game is the essence of a familiar premise. Remember when Barry Sanders suddenly retired from the Lions after the 1998 season at age thirty? Sanders's sudden departure remains one of sport's biggest mysteries of the last decade because no explanation ever given by Sanders ever seemed satisfactory. Besides, he had already rushed for 15,269 yards in his career and was probably a lock to set an NFL career-rushing mark, possibly even taking it to the 20,000-yard mark. Instead, Sanders stepped aside.

Which takes us back to Walker, who was the Brad Pitt–cover boy, Peyton Manning–athlete of his day, all in one. He was almost too good to be true, a great athlete with movie-star looks often acknowledged by teammates as the smartest guy on the field. Get this: his father was a high school teacher and football coach who, when Doak was born was asked if his son would someday become president, answered by saying, "No, he'll be an All-American."

Walker was that and more while starring at Southern Methodist University (SMU) in Dallas, which is where he grew up, a graduate of nearby Highland Park High School (where one of his teammates was future fellow Lions great Bobby Layne). Walker certainly wasn't big, even for a running back—five feet ten, 170 pounds—and on top of that, scouts would say that he was too slow to play pro football. How slow was he? Not slow enough. They didn't keep times for the forty in those days, but three times he was an All-American at SMU. He won the Heisman Trophy in 1948, finishing third in the voting in both 1947 and 1949.

Walker was such a draw at SMU that the school had to move its home games away from campus to the Cotton Bowl (which came to be known as the "House That Doak Built") on the far side of town to accommodate the crowds that came to see him play. The rest of the world got to see plenty of him, too. That's because he appeared on countless magazine covers, to include *Post, LIFE, Look,* the *Saturday Evening Post,* and later, *Sports Illustrated.* Interestingly, in the same year in which Walker appeared on the cover of *SI,* 1955, another athlete to adorn an *SI* cover was Olympic skier, Skeeter Werner—who later would become Walker's second wife. They would meet when Werner gave Doak skiing lessons at Steamboat Springs.

As great a player as Walker was in college, he was an even bigger star in the NFL, playing for the Lions. He would become a five-time All-Pro, pretty impressive considering he played only six seasons, on his own volition at that. In that time, Walker won a couple of league scoring titles as a runner, receiver, and kicker. His far-reaching skills conjure up names of other versatile players like him who would follow, such as Gino Cappellitti, Paul Hornung, and George Blanda. He helped lead the Lions to NFL titles in 1952 and 1953, and they would go back to the championship game in 1954, only to lose to the Cleveland Browns.

Perhaps the greatest compliment bestowed on Walker was that offered by the legendary sportswriter Grantland Rice, who described him as "the most authentic all-around player in football history."

Astute sports historians might even go so far as to compare Walker to another great sports figure of the twentieth century—golfer Bobby Jones. When Jones retired from competitive golf, right after he had won golf's then-version of the Grand Slam, he was only twenty-eight years old. Likewise, Walker was twenty-eight when he retired at the top of his game, following the 1955 season—certainly much too young by any era's standards. But Doak's sons, Russ and Scott, confirmed that their grandfather had told their dad "he needed to get out on top, be healthy, and be in business by the time he was thirty." Doak's dad simply didn't want him to be a has-been, as though that would have been a concern when reminded that in his six short years in the NFL, he was an All-Pro four times and went to five Pro Bowls.

It was about twenty years ago, in the mid-1980s, that I finally got to meet Walker, and he quickly struck me as being as kind and gentle as his reputation suggested. Believe it or not, my dad, even way up there in Canada, had been a huge fan of both SMU and Texas Christian University, and so it was only natural that I would come to think the world of the Doaker. My regard for him would only grow the more I got to know him.

Even though Walker retired from football not long after I was born, I can still get a sense of what the game was like when he was playing. It was an era when players played with God-given bodies not enhanced in a chemistry lab. It was a more intimate game in those days, with smaller, less-absorbent padding and helmets that lacked faceguards, where high-top shoes were in vogue. It was a somewhat slower game, less complicated, and the game's competitive extreme was more vicious than overtly violent.

It wasn't exactly a gentleman's game even then, but it was a sport in which gentlemen like Walker could excel without compromising their values or principles. It was more a game of masters and less of monsters. There is comparatively little film of the game from those days, and often what we are able to see are more snapshot snippets than thoroughly modern theatrics. Still, there's enough of it to see the football genius and savvy of Walker, who probably never received an order or instruction he couldn't follow, even if it meant banging helmet to helmet or losing a tooth here and there.

When I first met Walker, his alma mater had just been nailed by the NCAA, given the death penalty for a continued pattern of rules violations dating back several years. It was an embarrassing indictment of the school, leaving the university with obvious challenges in the months ahead.

Sometime after the NCAA doled out the death penalty to SMU, school vice president of development Bill Lively set about to rid the school of its negative stigma and restore it to its days of grace and glory, just like those it had experienced with Walker. Lively called me one day and asked if I would have lunch with him. It was at that meeting that Lively said he wanted to start a sports-luncheon series at SMU in which well-known sports figures, i.e., role models, would be brought in as keynote speakers. In telling me all this, Bill asked me what I thought of the idea, and if I was in favor, whether I'd join the Board of Trustees he was creating and serve as the master of ceremonies of the series. I thought the concept was great and his vision on target, and I jumped at the opportunity.

This connection would circle back around to include Walker a couple of years later, when Lively broached the subject of creating a college football running back of the year award that would be named after Walker. Stroke of genius. In the years since, the creation of new individual awards in various sports has become a cottage industry all its own. There's got to be veteran sports promoters kicking themselves for not beating Lively to the punch, attaching a name such as Walter Payton, Gale Sayers, Jim Brown, or O. J. Simpson (oops) to such an award back in the '70s or '80s and making hay with it.

Doak absolutely loved the idea of the award as soon as it was presented to him. He not only agreed to lend his name to the award but to do whatever was asked of him to help make it a meaningful special event. What I find almost as amazing about Walker as any of his on-field exploits was his ability to connect with people from all walks of life. We're talking about a guy who was making headlines before I was born, and yet when my son Doug met him decades later, Doug was totally drawn to Walker and vice versa. How much of an impact did Doak have on Doug? Doug has the rights to a movie about both Doak and Bobby Layne, which he hopes to have completed within the next year or so.

Such a film would certainly be uplifting and inspirational. Even into his seventies, Walker remained active in recreational sports for two reasons: he loved sports, and he loved doing things around the many people he cared about. In addition to skiing, he also was an avid golfer, hunter, fisherman, and horseback rider. Tragically, his participation in sports would lead to his untimely death.

In late January 1998, while skiing in Steamboat Springs—by now he was seventy-one—Walker hit a bad patch of terrain and suffered a horrific accident that left him paralyzed from the neck down. Nine months after the mishap, Walker passed away from complications resulting from his paralysis. After the accident, the hospitalized Walker received more than six thousand faxes as well as hundreds of letters and cards from well-wishers around the world. "We certainly knew our father was famous, but until then we had no idea how much people admired him," said Scott Walker, one of Doak's four children.

The best way for me to describe my feelings about Doak is to avoid the hyperbole. He simply enjoyed people and life. He was one of the most kind, caring, and thoughtful men I ever had the opportunity of knowing.

Yes, a man of great versatility; but more importantly, a man who was just a good guy.

XIV

JOHN WOODEN

PRINCIPLE

It's easy to have principles when you're rich.
The important thing is to have principles
when you're poor.

—Ray Kroc

J ohn Wooden and my dad are two of a kind. Both are caring and compassionate, and neither has much gray in his values. Gray in their hair? Well, sure, but not in terms of their convictions. They see life as a constant procession of choosing between right and wrong, where many people in today's society shirk having to define right or wrong, comfortable instead to dwell in the land of moral relativism.

America, and not just the world of college basketball, has been blessed by the fact that Wooden has lived well into his nineties. He still is as much an icon today as he was in the 1960s and 1970s, when he led the UCLA Bruins to ten NCAA titles in a twelve-year span, seven of those coming in a row (1967–73). How amazing is that? It's so amazing that since Wooden retired after the 1974–75 season, having won his last NCAA championship when UCLA beat Kentucky in the finals, no other coach has won more than three national crowns in those thirty-one years. Only Bob Knight at Indiana and Mike Krzyzewski at Duke have won as many as three in that time.

Wooden's records and numbers are dazzling. Starting in 1971 and ending in January 1974, his UCLA teams won eighty-eight straight games. No other school has come close to matching that streak. In fact, only one other school—Knight's Hoosiers in 1975–76—has managed to complete a single season undefeated. Wooden's teams had four 30–0 seasons and won nineteen conference championships, eight of which accompanied an undefeated conference mark. In twenty-seven seasons at UCLA, Wooden compiled a 620–147 record, making for an incredible winning mark of .808.

There's another dimension to Wooden that makes him a basketball legend among legends—he also was a terrific player. Long before he became known as "the Wizard of Westwood," Wooden was a star player at Purdue. He captained the Boilermakers to two Big Ten championships, and in 1932, while Purdue was putting together a season that would get them voted as national champions, Wooden was earning honors as college basketball's player of the year. How appropriate that the trophy awarded each year to college basketball's player of the year is now named after Wooden.

Among the many things I admired about Wooden early on was how he stayed so composed during games. He would stay seated near the end of the UCLA bench, a game program (at least that's what I think it was) rolled up in his hand as he conducted himself with restraint as well as with respect for the game. No showboating. No sideline tirades. From watching today's game, you would think that coaches get paid for however many minutes they stand and yell during a game, trying to micromanage their teams possession after possession. Not Wooden. He may have talked or even raised his voice at times at officials and players (from both sides), but I can't ever remember seeing him lose his composure or take center stage.

There must be so much about what Wooden taught and coached still present in today's modern game, but more than anything, Wooden to this day embodies a time when good basketball play stressed fundamentals. There were the bounce pass, the pick and roll, and rhythmic half-court offenses, where four or five guys touched the ball before it was shot. It was a game where rebounding position was earned with hustle and guile, not with brutality and cheating hands or forearms. It was a time of purity, practically, where good defense began with arms extended out or straight up and where coaches figured out the most efficient manner for utilizing the respective skills of all five men on the floor instead of constantly looking for isolation plays.

If nothing else, the brand of basketball in Wooden's era was a better game to watch.

Wooden won with dignity and sportsmanship, and he has long conducted himself in exactly the same manner off the court. Such focus. Such wisdom. His fifteen-step *Pyramid of Success* is a fixture on coaches' bookshelves/ desktops across the country. His quotes are words to live by. These are my favorites: "We so often get caught up in making a living that we forget to make a life." "Integrity is doing the right thing when nobody is watching." "Character is what you really are; reputation is merely what you are perceived to be."

Coach Wooden has touched my life several times, and that's in large part because he touched my son Doug's life. It was in the early 1980s that I took Doug with me to Cal Lutheran College in California, where the Dallas Cowboys held their training camp in those days. At the same time, Doug was going to spend a week on the other side of the campus at Wooden's basketball camp. Doug and his fellow campers would have lunch at the cafeteria from 11:00 a.m. to noon, and then the Cowboys would get the cafeteria from noon to 2:00 p.m., giving Doug and me a brief chance to catch up on the day. It was clear from day one that he was really enjoying the camp.

To this day, what Doug remembers most about that week—which also afforded him the chance to hang out with some of the Cowboys, such as Super Bowl MVPs Randy White and Harvey Martin—was meeting an icon like Coach Wooden. Not only was Wooden a terrific coach, the best of the best, he also came across like a grandfather to Doug, which goes to show just how caring Wooden was and how comfortable he made people feel.

When the week was over and Doug was saying his good-byes, he was struck by the fact that Coach Wooden remembered his name as they bade each other farewell. I took a keepsake picture of the moment. It brought back memories of the time that track-great Jesse Owens had remembered my name, despite the fact that six months had passed since we had initially met. One of the little things in life that makes a big difference.

Wooden's coaching was not only about mastering the big picture, it was about attending to the smallest details. One of the things he harped on with his players was making sure that they not only wore socks, but wore them correctly and with their shoelaces properly tied. He did this to help his players avoid getting blisters on their feet.

A man of principle? Consider the story of how Wooden ended up at UCLA instead of at Minnesota. After two seasons and a 44–15 record at Indiana Teachers College—later to become Indiana State, where a guy named Bird would play some thirty years later—Wooden was faced with having to make a choice between job offers from UCLA and Minnesota, either of which constituted a promotion.

Wooden would later say he was prepared to accept the Minnesota job, preferring to stay in the Midwest. But when Minnesota officials didn't call Wooden by a set deadline, he made contact with UCLA and accepted the job there instead. Minutes later, a Minnesota official called Wooden, apologizing for the delay, saying that a snowstorm had forced him to be late in calling. Having made his commitment to UCLA, Wooden stood by his decision to head west, and history was set in motion.

"If fate had not intervened, I would never have gone to UCLA," Wooden said.

Wooden kept his promise, even though it went against his personal preference. To him, there was no indecision or backpedaling. This was black and white. It was about principles.

One more Wooden virtue worth mentioning: perseverance. He didn't have instant success at UCLA after arriving in Los Angeles in 1948. In Wooden's first thirteen seasons, the Bruins went to the NCAA Tournament only three times, and each time failed to make it past the first round. It wasn't until 1962 that a Wooden-coached Bruins team made it to the Final Four, and two years later UCLA finally won its first national title under Wooden, beating Duke 98–83 to complete a perfect 30–0 season, the first of his four unblemished campaigns.

No doubt Wooden himself would cringe to hear his name and "perfect" mentioned in the same sentence, but I will say this: John Wooden is about as perfect a role model as anyone can possibly be.

MICKEY MANTLE

HEROISM

Real heroes are men who fall and fail and are flawed . . . but win out in the end because they have stayed true to their ideals and beliefs and commitments.

—Kevin Costner

Any kid who loves and follows sports has Walter Mitty–like dreams. They range anywhere from throwing the late-game pass that wins the Super Bowl, to sinking the eight-foot putt to beat Jack Nicklaus at the U.S. Open, to scoring the breakaway goal that wins the Stanley Cup. The true test of a sports lover's "If I could do anything" sports dream is if it sticks with you into adulthood. The one that has stayed with me for decades is as clear as a bell.

It's being at the plate at Yankee Stadium in the bottom of the ninth in game seven of the World Series, with the bases loaded and my team, the Yankees, trailing 3–0. I have a chance to win it all with a towering home run, just like the Mick would do. Doesn't matter who's pitching: Newcombe, Spahn, Marichal, Koufax. I wanted to be Mickey Mantle.

I wore No. 7 in Little League, Pony League, and American Legion ball. I even wore it later in life while participating in charity/celebrity softball games. I wouldn't have it any other way. Mickey Mantle was my hero, and he remains the source of the Walter Mitty dream that still burns inside of me. It doesn't matter how old I am or how long I will live, I still get to experience that daydream over and over as many times as I like, and no one can stop me. As my mother often said, "They're your dreams. Let them be big ones."

Unfortunately, by the time Mantle passed away in 1995, much of his legacy was tarnished by stories of his alcoholism and his legendary carousing, as revealed in Jim Bouton's landmark revelatory and unflattering book about baseball, *Ball Four*. Bouton was to baseball what Woodward and Bernstein were to the presidency: a myth debunker who unveiled flaws in our public figures far beyond what most of us had ever imagined. Until *Ball Four* came out and we read all about the shenanigans of the likes of Mantle and Billy Martin, what we knew about Mantle were pretty much his legendary accomplishments as a home run–swatting switch hitter and speedy center fielder whose career was cut relatively short by injuries.

As someone who grew up in the 1950s and 1960s with an idealized regard for the likes of Mantle and all major leaguers, it was tough to hear the truth about Mantle. The exposure of an athlete's life away from the field was, in those days, nothing like it is today. There was so much that we didn't know, and now that we do, we sometimes wish we had never been told.

As a kid, I would have been shocked to know that some of my favorite players smoked cigarettes, even in light of the fact that smoking among the masses was an acceptable part of life back then. This was before the surgeon general's warning started appearing on all cigarette packs. It pains me to think what kind of a player Mantle might have been had he never drunk or had he been a light drinker, at worst.

Even in light of all that, the Mick will forever be heroic to me for what he was able to accomplish between the foul lines. He was a great all-around player, and he always seemed to perform his best when the most was at stake. And it wasn't just because he played his entire career in the limelight of New York, where every accomplishment is treated as headline news for all of the country to see. It was because of *how* he did great things, not *where*.

In his prime and before his body started breaking down, the Mick was arguably the epitome of what a great baseball player should look and play like. He was "The Natural" long before Robert Redford was a Hollywood star. As a Yankees fan, much like two other well-known people of my generation—Bob Costas and Billy Crystal—I worshipped the Yankees and Mickey Mantle, believing he was not only the most well-rounded player in the game but the most heroic with his clutch, towering home runs, and almost impeccable play in the outfield. He was blond, handsome, fast, and powerful, with a gifted

physique and a homespun, middle-American upbringing that was more Chip
Hilton than Chip Hilton was.

In his heyday, Mantle was a rival of the "Say Hey" kid, fellow center
fielder Willie Mays, who through much of the 1950s shared top New York
billing with Mantle as a member of the Giants. More than thirty years after
both Mantle and Mays had left their playing careers behind, baseball fanat-
ics continued to debate one of baseball's biggest conundrums—who the best
center fielder of not just their generation but perhaps all of baseball history
really was. As much as I admired Mays as a ballplayer, Mantle always gets
the nod from me as the greatest baseball player, let alone center fielder, of
that generation.

My adoration of Mantle was practically an obsession. Just for the fun
of it, I sent Mantle an invitation to my high school graduation. He didn't
show up, but my consolation years later was being able to tell him all about
that, at that point on a friend-to-friend basis, and being able to chuckle with
him about it. When I told him about the shot-in-the-dark invite, he asked
me if I had gotten a response to the invitation. I told him I had received a
picture of him in return. He seemed satisfied with my answer; I certainly was
enthralled by the photo.

In those later years, with my being all grown up and Mantle living in
Dallas, I was able to see him often, and he was gracious enough to sign all
those Mantle baseball cards I had saved from my youth, including the one
that I had carried around for decades in my wallet, à la Costas. Every time he
signed one, Mantle, at the time long retired and his public reputation dam-
aged, would half-jokingly ask me, "Is this going to take their value down?"

Never!

Mickey Mantle will always be "Mr. Clutch" to me; that much is written in
stone. No matter what challenge he faced in a game, he would always make
things right with a homer, a great catch, or a stolen base on a pair of gimpy

legs that were a root cause of his shortened career, even though he did stick around long enough to hit 536 career home runs before retiring at age thirty-six after the 1968 season. On top of that, his last four or five seasons with the Yankees were pretty much mediocre, his leg injuries making him a shadow of the player he had once been. In one of sport's biggest "what ifs," one has to wonder how many career home runs Mantle would have hit had he maintained a reasonable level of health and played as long as Mays did (until age forty-two, retiring in 1973).

Consider this: Mays and Mantle broke into Major League Baseball in the same year, 1951 (both were born in 1931), and if you look at their respective stats through their first twelve seasons (Mays missed the 1953 season, so I used his stats through 1963, whereas Mantle's stop at 1962)—which is about the time that fluke injuries started taking a big bite out of Mantle's playing health—the numbers tell a story. In his prime, Mantle was every bit the equal of Mays, who since the death of Ted Williams has worn the unofficial title as greatest living baseball player. The Mick's hitting stats over his first twelve seasons were 404 home runs, 1,152 runs batted in, and a batting average of .309, compared to 406, 1,179, and .314, respectively, for Mays. While Mays's batting average was a bit higher than Mantle's, Mays also had more than five hundred more at bats than Mantle did over the same time. It's exactly half a century ago that Mantle captured the first of his three MVP Awards. And it's also exactly fifty years ago in the summer of 2006 that Mantle won the Major League Triple Crown. No player has done it since. (Carl Yastrzemski was the last American League Triple Crown winner in 1967. There has not been a National League Triple Crown winner since the Cardinals' Joe Medwick in 1937). Mantle also had no peer when it came to post-season play, having led the Yankees to twelve World Series and seven championships. To this day, he holds more individual World Series career records than any other player in baseball history: home runs (18), runs batted in (40), runs scored (42), extra base hits (26), and total bases (123), among others.

I got to know Mantle well enough to know he was never comfortable with celebrity. Many superstar athletes love the spotlight; not Mantle. His Hollywood good looks, competitive grit, and athletic prowess propelled him into a limelight that he never embraced. There was no escape, as there was no free agency in those days, and it would have been unheard of for the Yankees to let Mantle go in a trade. He was in New York, wearing Yankee pinstripes. Celebrity doesn't get much more high profile than that.

Sadness surrounded Mantle, both in terms of my regard for him and in his regard for himself. I remember him literally apologizing to me late in life for his not being the role model for me that, as a youngster, I had long regarded him to be. Really, he was quite shy, a bit rough around the edges, and given to bad language—lots of profanity. He never understood why people were so enamored with him.

Underneath it all, though, I knew he had a good heart, and I know how corny that sounds. Think what you want. I have a handful of photos of me with a few folks that I really looked up to while growing up, and they include Byron Nelson, Arnold Palmer, Jack Nicklaus, Gale Sayers, Nolan Ryan . . . and Mickey Mantle. Yep, the Mick is right there with them. Always will be.

Although Mickey and his family weren't always together, I did get to know his wife, Merlyn, and his boys in particular, David and Mickey Jr. It was David who called me to tell me that Mickey had died, reaching me in Austin, where I was covering the Dallas Cowboys training camp. David asked me if I would join the family for the funeral in Dallas. I was certainly honored and most appreciative, as the throngs of media that had gathered outside were not allowed in the church proper for the service. I sat right behind Joe Pepitone and Reggie Jackson.

Hanging over my desk in my study at home is a large signed painting of Mickey given to me by the Mantle family. It's right above an autographed baseball and a picture of Mick and me in the dugout at the opening of The Ballpark in Arlington (home of the Texas Rangers), now known as Ameriquest Field. A few years after Mickey's death, Merlyn and David invited me over to Merlyn's condo to show me some of the memorabilia she had saved, although much of it was gone, lost for posterity when he sold it while drunk or was conned out of it by some fast-talking opportunist.

No matter; I will always remember the good things about Mick as well as the great exploits. That's in part the magic of the Yankee pinstripes and a young boy's everlasting dream.

I'll never forget when he received the donated liver that gave him a little bit longer to live. He became a great spokesman for transplant organs. Because of him, I was inspired to get involved with that mission and for years played in a charity softball game that benefited the cause. Upon Mantle's death, those supporting organ-transplant donations rose 500 percent. Once again, the magic of the Mick was coming to life.

I will forever remember that hot August day over a decade ago, sitting in the church at Mantle's funeral as Bob Costas so eloquently delivered the eulogy, remembering the Mick: "He was a fragile hero to whom we had an emotional attachment so long and lasting that it defied logic. In the last year, Mickey Mantle, always so hard on himself, finally came to realize the distinction between a role model and a hero. The first, he often was not. The second, he always will be."

XVI

TIGER WOODS

MATURITY

To exist is to change, to change is to mature, to mature is to go on creating oneself endlessly.

—Henri Bergson

E ver since Tiger Woods turned pro in the fall of 1996, it's been almost impossible to take our eyes off him. He's that fascinating to watch, a great golfer and charismatic personality who has changed the face of the game. As hard as it is to believe, it's now been ten years since Woods left Stanford University to make the jump to the PGA Tour, where he quickly showed that his three consecutive U.S. Amateur titles were no fluke—he won twice on tour in 1996 and then came back the following April to win the first of his numerous green jackets at Augusta National.

Woods has made the time fly by because his has been a steady presence in the media. He's a consistent threat to win, someone who really hasn't had a serious slump in that time and has won dozens of events, oftentimes in dramatic fashion. Such as that time in 2005 when he eventually won his fourth Masters Tournament, beating Chris DiMarco in a play-off about an hour after holing out a green-side chip at No. 16 that was an instant classic. It shot about fifteen feet past the hole, made a bit of a loop, and rolled back down the slope toward the hole, ultimately hanging on the edge of the cup for a few seconds before tumbling in. Ever since then, it has been the most replayed golf shot seen on television.

As though following a child star on a long-playing TV sitcom, we can honestly say that we've seen Tiger Woods grow up before our eyes. It started back in 1978, when at the age of two he made his memorable national-TV debut on *The Mike Douglas Show*, walking out on stage and wowing the likes of fellow guest Bob Hope with his ability to put a swing, or at least a swipe, onto a ball. Years later at age fifteen, he would become the youngest U.S. Junior Amateur champion in history, and he would end up winning that event three straight years, just like he would then do at the U.S. Amateur.

Still, there would be some growing up to do on his part. About a month after winning the Masters for the first time in 1997, Woods came to Dallas, where he won the Byron Nelson Classic and then went across town to Fort Worth, where he shot rounds of sixty-seven, sixty-five, and sixty-four to get to fourteen under par and position himself for yet another tour victory. Except this time Woods faltered a bit down the stretch at Colonial, eventually finishing tied for fourth, three shots behind winner David Frost.

As well as he had played Colonial in the first three rounds, Woods obviously left there with a bad taste in his mouth because as of this writing, he has not returned to Fort Worth to play in the Colonial. For one thing, there was a segment of fans that didn't treat Woods very well that week; there were even some hints of racism. Another factor that might have dimmed Woods's Fort Worth experience was the golf course itself. It's a lush, old-school, traditional course with lots of doglegs and other bends, but it's the type of course that tends to take the driver out of the hands of big hitters—big hitters such as Tiger Woods.

For Woods, the 1997 Colonial boiled down to the last three holes, and, to put it bluntly, he fell apart. When it was over, Woods sequestered himself in the players' locker room and refused to talk to the media. It was a form of pouting that, at the time, didn't do much to enhance his image. He eventually bolted town and has not returned, at least not to play in the Colonial. There were other missteps in Woods's early years as a pro, such as the time he blew off an awards luncheon for college golfers at which he was scheduled to be the keynote speaker and other times where he pulled out of a tour event at the eleventh hour. As for Fort Worth, Colonial in recent years has been played opposite an event in Europe, where Woods gets a tidy guarantee and a good reason not to ride his horse back into Cowtown.

One thing you have to remember about Woods is that while he was quickly asserting himself as a dominant golfer in the late 1990s, he was still, basically, a college-aged kid, given to impulse, a small measure of immaturity (not having a full grasp of how his actions or decisions would be viewed by others), and youthful habits such as a hankering for fast food and video games enjoyed with his pals. Let's just say his first few years on tour were an adventure of highs, lows, rights, and wrongs. All this while living under a microscope, magnifying everything he did along the way.

In recent years, it appears as though Tiger has mellowed a bit and matured. Turning thirty (December 2005 for him) will do that for you. So will marriage, with Tiger's October 2004 wedding to the Swedish former nanny and swimsuit model Elin Nordegren. Woods has now won each major at least two times, including the Masters Tournament four times, and he regained his No. 1 world ranking after losing it for a while. Most recently, Woods was generally considered the leader of the pack of "the Big Five" that also included Phil Mickelson, Ernie Els, Vijay Singh, and Retief Goossen.

Cynics conjectured that when Woods got married, he would lose some of his edge, but it appears the other way around. He seems more relaxed, certainly more comfortable within himself, and more assured of the fact that when he gets it going on the golf course, many of the other top golfers in the world seem to cave, some more than others. In the ten years he has been on tour, Woods has "rebuilt" his swing twice, and in early 2006 he didn't rule out more reconstruction projects as time goes on, depending on the circumstances and what the sport is doing around him.

There's no question that, save for the occasional bum knee or back twinge, Woods is healthier now than he ever has been. His diet now is turbocharged, and years of serious training and workouts have sculpted a lean, mean physique in which he demonstrates that the man of the future is now. Watching him, you get a sense that he remains fiercely hungry and yet content at the same time, knowing there really isn't anything more to prove, except perhaps whether or not he can better Jack Nicklaus's career win record of eighteen professional majors or even catch up to the Golden Bear's proclamation that Woods would win the green jacket at least ten times before it's all over.

If Woods is ruthless, he is at least gracious in victory as well as in defeat. When he defeated John Daly in a playoff at the 2005 WGC American Express Championship, Woods acknowledged that he had been the beneficiary of a Daly misstep, a missed three-foot putt. As competitive and passionate as he is when it comes to wanting to win every tournament he enters, winning as the result of a friend's failing at a crucial time isn't what Woods lives for. He made that known publicly, and it didn't come across as an act of patronization. A similar thing happened soon thereafter at the 2006 Buick Invitational, this time involving Jose Maria Olazabal, who missed a gimme putt.

Watching an opponent falter is not the way Woods likes to win. Showing and expressing his empathy for an opponent who has just snatched defeat from the jaws of victory is evidence that Tiger has matured from the days of the public outburst or the stay-in-the-locker-room sulking. Woods has learned to win with humility, and that makes him a true champion.

This is why I think that as Tiger continues to mature, he will be able to enjoy each of his victories even more. In turn, golf fans will grow increasingly eager to support and cheer for someone who demonstrates a greater degree of gratitude and humility.

Maybe being married will help further ground him, allowing him to find a better balance in his life. At that point, he will become the consummate role model, not just for golf or even the world of sports at large, but for life as well.

We know that Tiger has matured because his rival peers say he has. Ernie Els, six years Woods's senior, said in the June 2006 issue of *Golf Magazine* that he has seen Woods grow from teenager to man, secure in who and what he is at age thirty. In a way, the world has seen Woods grow from the tot who appeared on *The Mike Douglas Show* to a rock-solid man—and husband now—mature and acutely aware of how he is viewed by the rest of the world and self-assured in how he conducts his business, both on and off the course.

At the time I was writing this book, Woods's father Earl passed away at age seventy-four, following a long illness that had confined him to his California home for much of the last year or so of his life. It is impossible to talk about Tiger Woods's life without exploring the prominent role Earl played in it. He introduced Tiger to the game of golf, but even more importantly, he instilled in his prodigy son the values and direction needed to perform as someone who could change the world through more than just his great golf.

Those who knew Earl well speak of how the latter was anything but a Little League parent, obsessing over his son's golf success at the expense of everything else in his life. While Earl was a mentor and sounding board for his son, it was Tiger who had the passion for the game of golf. His father merely guided him on the path to achieving his golf greatness without losing an awareness of what else was important in life: discipline and principles, gratitude and stewardship.

The relationship between dad and son in the Woods family is different, obviously, from the dad-son dynamic in my family, and yet they are so much alike. The strength of the bond between father and son, the way in which life lessons were carefully planned and then passed along over the years, and the goal to make a complete man out of the son, as concerned for his fellow man as he is for himself characterize both.

As heartbroken as Tiger must have been following the death of his dad, it is gratifying to know that they were able to share a love and mutual respect that survived Tiger's maturation from baby, to toddler, to boy, to young man, to world icon. The embrace that Earl Woods gave Tiger walking off the eighteenth green at Augusta, following Tiger's first Masters victory in 1997, was a special moment, especially for those of us who have time and again had the good fortune to share similar warm hugs with our own dads. For that, I do count my blessings.

And yet, I'm convinced that following Tiger's win in the 2006 British Open Championship, his first victory following the death of his dad, with tears streaming down his fatigued face, was the most meaningful display of love, admiration, and respect we have ever witnessed between Tiger and Earl Woods. "I'm kind of the one who bottles things up a little bit and moves on, tries to deal with things in my own way," said Woods, "but, at that moment it just came pouring out—all the things my father has meant to me—I just wish he could have seen it one more time." The world's greatest player on the world's greatest stage for all to see. And yet it was a part of Tiger that he's rarely ever shown or shared with the public.

And how ironic that Woods, on this day, would be paired in the final group with Chris DeMarco, who like Tiger had earlier in the month been forced to cope with the loss of a parent, having tragically lost his mother to a sudden heart attack. "I know my mom would be very proud of me right now," said DeMarco (who finished alone in second place, two shots behind Tiger), "one, for playing, but two just because that's how she was. I miss her and I love her and I have great memories of her and that's the hardest part. I know I'll never see her again. But, I know if I close my eyes, I see her. She is and was a wonderful woman." Despite the absence of his mother, DeMarco had convinced his own dad to come to England (and accompany Chris's young son) to watch the tournament. It no doubt did wonders, as the grieving and long healing process continued for the entire DeMarco family.

The fact that with his win Woods tied Walter Hagen for second place on the all-time list for career wins in major tournaments (only seven behind Jack Nicklaus's eighteen), often takes a back seat to the emotion of that day.

The '06 British Open was about two golfers matched together in the final round of the oldest golf tournament in the world. After the heat of the battle, only one would remain the victor. Yet despite their competitive spirit, the two shared a common bond, while a worldwide audience of millions looked on, touched and overcome by their genuine outpouring of emotion. "He would have been very, very proud," said Tiger of his dad.

The drama of athletic competition had given way to the true, raw, human emotion of real life.

The lasting relationship between a dad and his son had taken center stage. "I love my Dad and I miss him very much," said Woods. And as I watched Tiger lift the Claret Jug high over his head, I couldn't help but think that what I was seeing is what this book is all about. And there it was, coming to life before my very eyes.

XVII

JOHN ELWAY

SELFLESSNESS

There is no limit to what can be done if it doesn't matter who gets the credit.

—Author Unknown

There is so much to say about John Elway that it's hard to know where to start. Let's begin with the fact that he wore No. 7 as Denver Broncos quarterback. As any true sports fan would know, that was the same number that my hero, Mickey Mantle, wore as a New York Yankee. Lucky seven. Lucky me, that I got to know both guys.

It's not often that I have found myself impressed with sports figures younger than me, but Elway is one of the few exceptions, and it's because of a powerful father-son connection. On a couple levels. The more I have gotten to know Elway, the more I know that he fits my dad's standard of a sports figure who has great character and is worthy of admiration, much like the relationship John had with his dad. There's also the connection that involves my own son, Doug, who since he was a little guy has idolized Elway as his favorite sports hero. More on that shortly.

The most dominant aspect of Elway's character, to me, has always been his selflessness, how he puts others before himself, even strangers he meets and greets at a charity function or some other kind of event. He does not use his celebrity as a free pass to get out of his off-field commitments or to shorten his time pressing the flesh with the "common folk." In fact, he seems to cherish those times he gets to meet fans and admirers. Either that, or he is the world's greatest actor.

Long before Elway was leading the Broncos to a pair of Super Bowl victories in the 1990s, he was winning the hearts of nearly everyone with whom he came in contact. Such was the case back in the mid-1980s, when I was emceeing a Girls Club of Dallas function sponsored by Nestlé. Elway was a spokesman for Nestlé, so he was there too, and it was clear that he was there to do much more than just punch his ticket.

It was the first time I had met him away from the football field, and he was unbelievable. He had time for everyone, whether it was corporate types, sponsors, parents, or kids—even the media. Sure he was likely being paid handsomely, but there was nothing about Elway that gave a hint of ego. He was simply gracious and down-to-earth.

Before going to the function, I had called ahead to Nestlé to ask them if I could bring along a young, wheelchair-bound boy who idolized John, knowing it would mean the world to him if he got the chance to meet Elway. Three-year-old Tommy had muscular dystrophy, and I had met him and his family through my years co-hosting the Jerry Lewis Labor Day Telethon. Even though the Nestlé folks told me it would be fine, I still had no assurance that Elway would go along with all of this. I even told Tommy and his parents not to get their hopes up too high, that I would do my best to work things out, but no promises. They understood and were just excited to be able to get the chance to go.

What happened next practically blew my mind, having been down this road before with some athletes. When I introduced Tommy to his idol, John got down to his knees to eye level with Tommy, and they went one-on-one, genuinely bonding. It couldn't have gone any better, and that's not even the best part of the story. They have stayed in touch over the years. When Tommy graduated from high school five years ago, he got a graduation package in the mail, sent by Elway. It was a large Waterford crystal replica of the Denver Broncos stallion, with Tommy's name on it. Most people will never know about this great example of a high-profile athlete like Elway making a difference in the life of a child. But Tommy sure does.

There's a similar story involving my own son, Doug, and this one comes without the stage of a special event like the one that brought Elway and Tommy together. This happened more by chance. Doug was fourteen at the time. With the Cowboys about to play the Broncos in a preseason game at Mile High Stadium in Denver, the Cowboys were kind enough to issue Doug a sideline photo pass so that he could accompany me to the game as a grip, with the ultimate prize being an up-close glimpse of Elway.

In a roundabout way, Doug's adoration of Elway actually dates back to when he was only about three or four years old, before Elway had even gone to Stanford, let alone the Broncos. While still working in D.C., I covered Super Bowl XII between the Cowboys and Broncos in New Orleans. Being that I was a lifelong New York Giants fan (thus a Cowboys "hater" almost by necessity), when it came time to pick out a souvenir from the game to take home to Doug, I picked a bright orange hat that had "Orange Crush" on it.

Bright orange immediately became little Doug's favorite color, which I supposed paved the way for him to connect so well with Elway when he ended up with the Broncos several years later. As Doug grew up to know better, he would come to admire Elway for more important things, like his grit and tenacity, as well as his being so big and strong, with a gun for an arm. Doug collected every Elway trading card, picture, and poster he could get his hands on.

Fast forward to that Cowboys-Broncos preseason game at Mile High, with Doug along with me on the trip. Doug must have taken fifty photos of Elway during the game, and it certainly didn't bother him one bit that the Broncos won the game. When it was over, I had to do a thirty-minute, live postgame show back to Texas, so Doug asked me if during that time he could saunter over to the Broncos locker room and perhaps catch a glimpse of Elway. I told him to be careful and polite, to not do anything that would get him (and therefore me) in trouble.

Off he went to the Broncos locker room, eventually getting cleared by the security guard to go in. When Doug entered, as he would tell me later, he noticed that most of the players had left, except for Elway, who was by his locker, putting on his brown bomber jacket. He then noticed Doug and started up a conversation with him. My son told him how he had always been the one guy he looked up to and respected.

Elway looked at Doug and noticed the camera and about a half dozen pictures of Elway under Doug's arm, and on the spot he asked Doug if those photos needed to be signed. After signing all the photos while maintaining a conversation with Doug, Elway called over the security guard and asked him if he wouldn't mind taking a photo of him with his new pal, Doug Murray.

That picture sits proudly on Doug's bookshelves alongside all the autographed posters, and to this day, he still describes that encounter with Elway as one of the most memorable moments of his life. It certainly was evident at the time; as Doug walked back across the field to link back up with me, the ear-to-ear grin told me that he was pretty much walking on air.

Another story about Elway that speaks volumes about what kind of guy he is concerns his induction into the Pro Football Hall of Fame in Canton, Ohio. Most inductees will ask someone like a former head coach or teammate to introduce them at the ceremony, but Elway displayed a different tack, one truly from the heart—he had his daughter Jessie do the honors. It was a brilliant and memorable move. Jessie elicited both tears and laughter from the crowd with her storytelling, and John, I'm sure, enjoyed the moment as much as he had enjoyed any moment in his life. Ditto for Jessie.

It's amazing how things came full circle involving me, Elway, and my son, Doug—all because of a bright-orange cap I bought my son years before Elway even got to the Broncos. This is a guy who despite being adorned with the tag of "greatest active player never to have won the Super Bowl" for all those years before winning those two Super Bowls, always went out of his way to make a difference in people's lives simply by taking a moment, just as he had done with Tommy and Doug. And, guess what? He still is going out of his way.

Elway has taken his economics degree from Stanford and become the consummate businessman as a restaurant owner, owner of multiple car dealerships, television corporate spokesperson, creator of his own line of furniture, and now a team owner of the Colorado Crush in the Arena Football League. As for Tommy, he's now twenty-three years old and a sports marketing graduate from Texas A&M. Amazing, considering his parents didn't expect him to live long enough to even enter kindergarten. But medical science and an incredible will to live have changed that in the twenty years since I first introduced Tommy to Elway. So, fast forward once again. Tommy, like every college grad, looking for that first job in the real world six months ago, sent out letters and résumés to teams from the NHL, NBA, NFL, Major League Baseball, and the Arena Football League, including Elway's Crush.

Now, you'd have thought Tommy might have pulled a few strings and taken advantage of his relationship with Elway, but instead he simply sent his résumé to the team's general address. Yet, as fate would have it, an assistant in the Crush's corporate offices recognized Tommy's name and showed it to Elway. Next thing you know, John's on the phone with Tommy, inviting him to join the Crush. Within days, Tommy and his mom were off to Denver, where Tommy was to use his sports management degree to assist with advertising, marketing, PR, sales, and special events. Elway welcomed him at his first daily staff meeting with a simple, "Please welcome Tommy everybody. He's my new right-hand man." (Tommy's wheelchair would be parked to John's immediate right for the remainder of his stay.) Six months later, Tommy returned to Dallas to get ready to begin law school at SMU, but not before John (who was now even more impressed with Tommy's great knowledge and ability) assured him he'd have a job waiting for him whenever he was ready to return to Colorado. In the interim, the team linked Tommy up from his home in Dallas to their Colorado offices so he could continue his work via computer on the team's media guide and the Crush Web site during the off-season.

Quite a story. It's a relationship that initially began by a chance meeting yet now, two decades later, has grown into a lifelong friendship. One that has kept alive the hopes and dreams of a physically challenged young boy well into young adulthood. Reflecting on the selfless difference Elway has made in the lives of those like young Tommy easily brings back memories of just how great a competitor Elway was on the football field. He was the kind of leader you'd want to go to war with, a never-give-up kind of guy who set an NFL career record with forty-seven come-from-behind victories or game-tying comebacks.

Amusingly enough, he's also the answer to an interesting trivia question: Who was the losing quarterback in the unforgettable Stanford-Cal game when the Stanford band came on the field too early in the closing seconds, allowing the Bears to lateral their way to a fluke winning touchdown as time ran out? You guessed it: John Elway.

I also get a kick out of the fact that coming out of Stanford, Elway, also a stud baseball player, was drafted by my beloved New York Yankees. He was also drafted as the No. 1 pick in the NFL draft by the Colts, who then traded him to Denver. That was the same year that his college roommate, baseball third baseman Steve Buechele, would be drafted by the Texas Rangers, and this was soon after I had arrived in DFW to begin work there. Steve would become a good friend—he and his wife, Nancy, are to this day—and he has never stopped talking about how special a guy John Elway is: driven, focused, positive, and selfless. He's just good people.

Obviously, I'm not the only one who feels that way.

XVIII

PAT SUMMERALL

PROFESSIONALISM

*Professionalism: it's not the job you do,
it's how you do the job.*

—Author Unknown

T here are the quiet times in life when I can sit back on the sofa and, with the TV turned off, close my eyes and relive in my mind flashbacks of great sporting events that I have been witness to over the years. I can picture the great plays, see the unforgettable moments, and instantly tap into the very same emotions I experienced twenty, thirty, forty, even fifty years ago, when television was in its infancy.

That's the beauty of being in love with sports—the ability to cling to wonderful memories that, in truth, are journeys in sound as much as they are experiences in sight. And for anyone who has followed sports, especially football, over the last thirty or forty years, there are two voices in particular that stand out from all the rest.

Theirs are the voices that come as close to God's as a man's can get because of their innate ability to evoke the passions of the game in ways that were restrained yet unmistakably authoritative. One of those great voices was silenced years ago; the other recently retired from the game, a deep, melodic, voice that will forever be associated with CBS's glory years of televising NFL football.

The former voice belongs to someone whose face is unknown to most: that's the incomparable John Facenda, for many years the voice of NFL Films, who turned replay shows into Cecil B. De Mille spectacles. But when I experience those cherished moments of closing my eyes and seeing/hearing the call of the games themselves, the voice I hear more than any other is the one that belongs to the ageless Pat Summerall.

Whether it was describing another Dallas Cowboys fourth-quarter comeback on a brisk, overcast Thanksgiving Day when the turkey, stuffing, and all the other works were *finally* moving along to make room for the pecan pie or chocolate cake, or aptly calling Jack Nicklaus once again charging over the back nine at Augusta to win another Masters, Pat Summerall to me epitomized the sports-viewing experience.

As much as Pat is a pal to me, it is his long career as a sports announcer—a career that literally spans my life from childhood, to manhood, to middle age, to AARP status—that means so much to how I define the sports world in which I live. It is why, when I really think about it and dig deep into my memories of living sports, Summerall exists as a sort of surrogate father to me, someone who was always there for me, tending to me sight unseen, sometimes from thousands of miles away. Other than my precious dad, if ever there was anybody I admired for his ability to make a sports event and our heroes who participated come to life, it was Pat Summerall.

At least in most respects, and I'll get into that later.

Before I became a sportscaster, while I was still in college, I was intent on becoming a pediatrician. I regarded sports and broadcasting more as side-lights, hobbies, and avocations than the cornerstones to what would become my chosen profession. I never thought I could make a living in television sports and news. It was fun stuff that fascinated me, but being an MD work-ing with kids was what I really took seriously.

Like anybody else who loved sports, I had my favorite sportscasters, and it's a list that has grown over the years. As a boy, my favorites were Mel Allen, Jim Simpson, Jim McKay, Curt Gowdy, Vin Scully, Keith Jackson, and Jack Buck. I have since come to know and admire many more sports-casters, thanks to my job.

There's Verne Lundquist of CBS, who's as versatile a play-by-play announcer as anyone. He left the DFW ABC affiliate close to twenty-five years ago, but he and his wife, Nancy, remain dear friends.

Then there's Bill Macatee. I remember when he came into the broadcast business over twenty-five years ago. We worked for competing stations but became instant friends and have stayed in touch, even though Bill is now with CBS and the USA Network. One of today's most popular TV men and certainly one of the most competent is Jim Nantz of CBS. In fact, I tried to get him to come work with me in Dallas when he got out of college in Houston, but another station beat me to the punch. It pleases me to no end to see the success he continues to enjoy. There's ESPN's Chris Berman, truly one of the real characters in our business, who makes it fun. Another of my favorites is *NFL Today* on CBS host James Brown, a smart, thoughtful, down-to-earth, good guy who I met more than twenty-five years ago when we both were working in Washington, D.C. And certainly, Bob Costas. He's always prepared, intelligent, and quick-witted, and he commands great respect for his versatility. Bob gets it. He has few peers, as he's rock solid at every broadcast event he's involved with.

Yet, when I finally decided to forego my original career choice of pediatrician, it was probably because of the two men on my short list, ultimate professionals whose talent and appeal have transcended several generations. I'm talking about Pat Summerall and Dick Enberg. They have always been committed, creative, and consistent, as they both have this incredible knack for making you feel like you are there and part of the action, no matter what the event.

I met Dick years ago through our mutual association with NBC as well as covering or attending events. I even substituted for him one year as the master of ceremonies at his annual GTE College Academic All-American awards program. I first heard of Dick in the late 1960s, when he did the famous UCLA-Houston basketball game featuring Lew Alcindor (aka Kareem Abdul-Jabbar) and Elvin Hayes. This was back when he was the voice of the California Angels. That's close to forty years ago, and, yet, four decades later, he's still as sharp (has a PhD in education), creative, descriptive, accomplished, and, to use his trademark Enberg phrase, "oh my," so eloquent with whatever, wherever, and whenever he might be broadcasting.

Bill Walsh, the former San Francisco 49ers head coach and longtime broadcast partner of Enberg's once told me, "Dick is simply the best. Always wears his heart on his sleeve."

Ironically enough, I was the master of ceremonies last year when Enberg received the Pat Summerall Award for excellence in broadcast journalism.

Which brings me back to Pat Summerall, who excelled at letting the event do the talking. In his mind, brevity was best; he belonged to the old school of "less is more." Pat has told me on several occasions that he wasn't consciously speaking less, counting his words or doing anything like that. It just came out that way, as Pat thought it best to just let what was happening on the field speak for itself.

The thing about Summerall is that there was nothing bombastic about the way he called a game. Not even close. His was a knack difficult to teach: he could raise the excitement level of his commentary without raising his voice. He didn't so much call play-by-play as he did set the scene like a movie narrator: a last name here, a verb phrase there, a simple declaration of a play's result. "Staubach . . . rolling left . . . throwing toward the end zone . . . Pearson, diving, makes the catch . . . TOUCH—down, Cowboys!" Then again, all those years alongside the booming, nonstop analysis of John Madden might have reinforced in Summerall the value of speaking only when necessary. However he did it, he was the best. Always the preeminent professional.

Pat once shared an interesting story with me, and to him it was words to the wise. Prior to Pat's first Masters Tournament, CBS golf producer Lance Barrow told him that he didn't want him saying, ". . . and he sinks the putt."

Pat went on: "Lance said, 'If you do, it'll be the last time you say it, because you'll be gone.' He told me the viewers aren't stupid; they can see [the golfer] make the putt." That's television; it's a visual medium. It's not like radio, where you're required to describe what's taking place at each moment.

Pat's soothing, deep, authoritative voice didn't hurt his credibility as a broadcaster, but he's so much more than just a voice. Anyone under the age of forty probably doesn't realize this, but Pat Summerall isn't just one of those talking heads who went straight from "broadcasting school" to a spot on network TV. He's one of the first "ex-jocks" who carried his success on the field to in front of the camera. He played professional football for nearly a decade, first as a place-kicker and tight end for the Chicago Cardinals from 1952 through 1957, then finishing his nine-year career playing for the New York Giants from 1958 through 1961, a stint which gave him the chance to play in three NFL Championship games, including the classic 1958 overtime loss to Johnny Unitas and the Baltimore Colts.

Summerall began his career with CBS on a part-time basis in 1960. At the time, Pat was rooming with Giants teammate, quarterback Charlie Conerly. CBS called Charlie one day to set up an appointment for an audition. However, as fate would have it, Charlie was in the shower when the phone rang, so Pat answered it. The representative from CBS was so impressed with Pat's voice that he invited Pat to come in for an audition as well. The rest, as often said, is history. Pat was hired and would eventually become the network's signature voice, mainly for its coverage of the NFL and golf, to include the Masters, but also for events such as U.S. Open tennis, the NBA, and five heavyweight championship fights. From 1960 to 1971, he was the sports director of WCBS Radio in New York, and he would later team with Madden for seventeen years as perhaps the greatest two-man broadcasting team in sports history.

I can remember how, when I was a kid, my dad would rave about Pat Summerall, how good he was, and how he would let the event tell its own story. He was never bigger than the story he was reporting, much like the legendary voice of the Packers' Ray Scott, whom Pat worked alongside in the early years. A true professional.

I grew up watching and listening to Pat Summerall—that unmistakable voice that seemed forever present on my TV. The first chance I got to meet him was in the 1970s while at the Atlanta airport, waiting to catch the hop to Augusta, home of the Masters Tournament. Years later, Pat would tell me that the most emotional event he ever covered was the 1986 Masters, the one at which forty-six-year-old Jack Nicklaus scorched the back nine on Sunday to become the oldest winner of the green jacket. Pat said as he watched Jack and his caddie son Jackie walk up eighteen, he could see the tears rolling down the cheeks of his broadcast partner, Ken Venturi, and feel his own tears starting to meander down his cheeks. He was so choked up, he couldn't speak. Again, brevity would serve him well, although he really had no choice in this instance.

Another of Summerall's longtime broadcast partners was Tom Brookshier, who joined Summerall for many years in the CBS booth doing NFL telecasts. Together, Brookshier and Summerall worked hard and lived even harder, doing their share of partying and drinking. Eventually, that pattern of alcohol excess would catch up with Summerall, so much so that it took an intervention from Brookshier along with Pat's family to get him to seek help for his alcohol problem, which he did at the Betty Ford Center. He has been sober ever since and has accepted Jesus Christ and Christian teachings in his life. He regularly shares his story to groups anxious to hear what he has to say.

As good a friend as Pat is, and as much as I found his competence behind the mike nearly impeccable, there's no way to sugarcoat how Pat messed up his life with alcohol. This is a profession that lends itself to ample amounts of socialization away from the broadcasting booth, and the temptations are many. In terms of drinking, there rarely comes a time that a refill isn't at arm's length, and the ability to stay sober requires the ability to say no and walk away. On those counts, Pat is the first to admit that he failed, and it nearly killed him.

More than once I've joined Pat and introduced him to attentive audiences. His message is real: it's about making good choices; it's about giving back; it's about respecting yourself.

It's about real life.

One person that he helped very much was another sports icon, his longtime pal, Mickey Mantle. They had gotten to know each other while they were in New York at the same time for a number of years. They were good friends, and their relationship remained intact through the years. In fact, it was Summerall who helped convince the Mick that he needed professional help for his alcohol problem, and Mantle would also end up going to the Betty Ford Center. It prolonged Mantle's life, but it didn't save him.

Pat has been more fortunate. He was given a second chance two years ago when he received a new liver. It gave him a new life.

Being a neighbor of Pat's, I get to see him and his supportive wife, Cheri, on a fairly regular basis. They are always anxious to help with charitable causes. It was at one of those events that I got to introduce Pat and my dad to each other. It was a very special moment for my dad. Understandably, for me too. These opportunities to "complete the circle" for my dad and me remain some of the most precious memories I will ever have, just as it was when I got him onto the ice at Boston Garden taking pictures, or when we went to Yankee Stadium and he walked onto the field like a child about to meet Santa Claus, immediately going to first base where his boyhood idol, Lou Gehrig, had become a Hall of Famer.

Pat fully realizes that some of the adversity in his life was self-inflicted. He has acknowledged and accepted responsibility for his actions, and he has challenged himself to get it right. He doesn't hide his gratitude for getting this second chance at life and remains humbled by the new opportunity at life he's been given.

It's been a privilege to get to know Pat over the years and to call him a treasured friend. His presence and that unmistakable voice will forever be linked with many of the greatest sports events of the past fifty years. Most importantly, I simply cherish the stories he is always willing to share, his wisdom that just permeates the air, and his friendship that I wouldn't trade for anything.

Being a pediatrician certainly is a worthy calling, but I'm quite happy with the career direction I took. It gave me the chance to meet and get to know professionals like Pat Summerall. There are few, so it doesn't get much better than that.

DOROTHY HAMILL

RESILIENCY

The pessimist sees the difficulty in every opportunity; the optimist sees the opportunity in every difficulty.

—L.P. Jacks

As a kid in my mid-twenties, I had figure skater Dorothy Hamill pegged as someone who had it all. She was her generation's "It" girl. What red-blooded male in America didn't feel the same way? She was a successful athlete and an Olympic gold medalist who was as cute as they come, with a style and a smile that were an unbeatable combination.

Half the men in America had a crush on her; the other half lied about it.

Her trademark wedge haircut, "the Dorothy 'do," was the talk of every frat house in the country. Overnight, she had become a fashion trendsetter, gracing the covers of magazines, appearing on TV shows all over the place, and simply capturing the hearts of Americans as a whole—men and women, boys and girls. Hamill transcended the sport of ice skating and became a global icon, much in the same way that Peggy Fleming, another American skating sweetheart, had eight years earlier in 1968.

Hamill had charm, dignity, and unparalleled grace, and she was an exciting skater to boot with a nice mix of athleticism and finesse, her trademark "Hamill camel" enthralling skating fans to no end. It was like she could do no wrong, yet through it all she seemed unaffected by her celebrity and all the hullabaloo around her.

It would be years later that we would learn that Hamill's world was far from perfect, even though she would become the first female athlete to sign a $1-million-a-year contract (with the Ice Capades) and would later break hearts across America with her seemingly idyllic marriage to Dean Paul Martin, the dashing and talented son of legendary entertainer Dean Martin. It turned out to be a house of cards, as Dorothy and Dino divorced. He would later die in a plane crash.

There also came a time in the mid-1990s that Hamill would have to declare bankruptcy, mainly the result of a failed business venture that involved co-ownership of the Ice Capades. "Money is evil," Hamill was quoted as saying in 1996, the year she filed for bankruptcy. About this time she was going through a second divorce, this time from Dr. Kenneth Forsythe, whom she accused of being unfaithful through much of their marriage.

When you gazed in admiration at Hamill atop the medals podium at the 1976 Winter Olympics in Innsbruck, you couldn't help but think she was on top of the world, a self-assured young woman in charge of her destiny and the envy of every woman who wanted to be in her lace-ups. Truth is, getting to that podium had never been a sure thing with Hamill—at least not in her mind.

How she got there was a study in resiliency, an ability to bounce back from setbacks, even if she were her own worst enemy. There is an old saying that it's not the number of times you get knocked down in life that determines who you are, but how many times you get back up. And if the latter number keeps up with the former, you're doing okay. In Hamill's case, she has done more than just "okay" with her ability to bounce back.

As hard as it might be to believe, self-esteem had never been Hamill's strong suit growing up. If anything, she had an almost total lack of self-confidence, a flaw that renowned skating coach Carlo Fossi would discover when he started coaching her full-time in the early 1970s. What Fossi discovered when he first took Hamill under his tutelage was not a savvy competitor bucking to be the best in the world, but a teenage girl suffering from stage fright and burdened with a bad case of self-deprecation. As sweet and self-assured as Hamill would appear years later in an Olympic ice rink, her apprenticeship under first Gus Lussi and then Fossi would be a years-long exercise in overcoming her rampant insecurity. Triple axels and double toe loops were a piece of cake compared to all the rest of it.

"Dorothy had a strong handicap in that she was negative," Fossi, now deceased, would say years later. "She had to be pushed and always said she couldn't win in competition. She was her own worst enemy."

Even Hamill herself weighed in with a retrospective self-analysis that was brutally candid, calling herself a spoiled brat who couldn't think for herself and was given to terrible tantrums, someone who, she said, "needed a swift kick in the pants."

Under Fossi, Hamill's skating swiftly matured, taking her from the days when she said she looked like a pretzel while training and performing to a genuine ice princess who could impress the judges at the same time she was dazzling the fans, making her first big move when she finished runner-up to 1972 Olympic bronze medalist Janet Lynn at the 1973 U.S. Nationals. A year later in Providence, Rhode Island, it was Hamill's turn. She won the first of three consecutive U.S. Nationals, culminating in her 1976 victory at Colorado Springs that sent her to Innsbruck as a member of the U.S. Olympic team. As we all know, the best was yet to come.

Still, Hamill was not the favorite headed to Innsbruck, although she was in the thick of the hunt for a medal, possibly bronze, or maybe even silver if she could perform superbly. In the pecking order of things, she fell in somewhere behind East Germany's Christine Errath and the Netherlands' Dianne de Leeuw, who, respectively, had won the 1974 and 1975 world championships, with Hamill finishing second both times.

On the Innsbruck ice, though, Hamill was near flawless, with all her 5.8s and 5.9s in both technical merit and artistic interpretation earning first place on all of the judges' cards. That was good enough to win the gold. The Dorothy 'do was a go. For good measure, Hamill won the world championship a month after winning her gold medal. "In some ways, this victory meant more to me than any other," Hamill said of her victory at the worlds in Sweden. "I won the Olympics for my country, but I won the world championship for myself."

The rest of 1976 for Hamill was like serving a year's reign as Miss America: a huge homecoming celebration that included a parade; adorning the cover of *Time* magazine; signing a multi-year contract with the Ice Capades; appearing in TV commercials, most notably with Clairol as a spokesperson/model for their Short & Sassy conditioner; her own TV special on ABC; and being swamped with cards and letters, many of them containing impromptu marriage proposals from eligible males—and likely a few ineligible males, unbeknownst to their wives.

It would be great to say that she lived happily ever after, but obviously that was not the case. Relationships and finances were not her only problems. Soon after turning forty, in 1996, she was diagnosed with osteoarthritis, a deterioration of joint cartilage, which showed up early with symptoms that involved loss of strength and stamina, leaving her with days in which it was all she could do to just pull herself out of bed in the morning. Plus, she ached all over.

It must have been around this time, in the mid-1990s, that I had the chance to meet Hamill, and there was nothing about how she conducted herself that let on that she was suffering physically, emotionally, or financially. The occasion was when she brought her skating company to Dallas to perform there. For her visit, I had planned a segment for my *Scott's Kids* program in conjunction with Big Brothers Big Sisters. I set it up so that Dorothy would teach a young Hispanic boy how to skate, and it was clear for everyone to see that this boy had never been on ice before, at least not with skates laced to his feet.

This is the Dorothy Hamill I will remember as much as the Olympic podium Dorothy of twenty years earlier. Her patience in working with this young boy was jaw-dropping. She showed him everything she could to help alleviate his fears, and when she took the boy by the arm to lead him around the ice, supporting him the whole way, I can assure you that every other male over the age of eight in that rink was gritting his teeth in envy. After the skating lesson, Hamill stuck around for the longest time, signing things, talking with people, posing for pictures, and doing an interview with me, even though she had a show to put on that very night. It was like she had nothing else to do, as though we were making her day and not the other way around.

Despite all the bumps and disappointments in her life—by the way, she responded quite well to the medications doctors gave her to treat her osteoarthritis; so much so, in fact, that she returned to the ice to skate in the 2000 Goodwill Games in her early forties—Hamill has always cleared her calendar to dive into charity work. One of her pet causes has been AIDS, and it doesn't stop there: the American Cancer Society, the Special Olympics, the March of Dimes, the President's Council on Physical Fitness, blind children and organizations that aid are among those she works with.

Thirty years have passed since Dorothy Hamill won an Olympic gold medal, and she is almost as popular now as she was then. Her guest appearance as a judge on *American Idol* made entertainment news around the world, in part because of the sexy top she was wearing, but also because it showed how enduring her appeal is, just as it has been for Peggy Fleming before her, making them two of the most gracefully aging, attractive, former Olympic gold medalists in the world.

To go through what she has gone through, while thriving and not just surviving, is a testament to what must be a strong will. Even if there is some small part of her that still deals with self-esteem issues, she more than offsets that with her ability to focus and discipline herself to achieve whatever she sets her mind to. On top of that, she is the consummate package of inner and outer beauty. America's Sweetheart, perhaps? She gets my vote.

It'll be interesting to watch her for the decades to come, because I've got to believe she's got a whole new set of goals she plans on accomplishing. Stay tuned.

TOM LANDRY

FAITH

Without faith, nothing is possible.
With it, nothing is impossible.

—Mary McLeod Bethune

If they ever make a Mount Rushmore for sports legends, Tom Landry's visage goes up there first.

The legendary Dallas Cowboys coach was "the Great Stoneface," a living, breathing, stoic statue who commanded the Cowboys sideline for twenty-nine years, leading the franchise to 270 victories—third-most all-time in the NFL—and appearances in five Super Bowls, two of which they won. On top of that, Landry was a man of principles, virtues, and strong Christian faith, the consummate sports role model if ever there was one.

Faith begins with the belief that there is something, or someone, greater than oneself. It is, to a Christian, a belief in something not seen, in that we "live by faith, not by sight," as it says in 2 Corinthians 5:7. Landry never hid the fact that he was a man of Christian faith, committed to a God who asks of His followers not to defend Him but to proclaim Him. And that, Landry did.

The importance of Landry's faith in this context is not to say that his faith was better or truer than anyone else's. It's to make the point that as successful as he was coaching football and leading men, the sport did not occupy the top spot on his personal ladder of priorities. It was down on a rung somewhere below his love of God and love of family, and that faith never wavered when crowded by worldly success on one side and man's rampant cynicism on the other. Landry stuck to his faith through times when it was unpopular to do so and at other times when it was fashionable to go around wearing it on one's sleeve.

Landry was a man of conviction, the epitome of someone, "who said what he meant and meant what he said." Star running back Tony Dorsett found this out the hard way during his rookie season, when he had made arrangements for his entire family—his mother, father, sisters, and brothers—to make the trip from Pennsylvania to Texas to see him play in a game. Only problem was, he almost didn't play.

"Just before the game, Coach calls me into his office and tells me I'm not going to start," Dorsett told me. "He said I might not even play because I had missed a light practice the day before. I looked straight into his eyes and he looked straight back into mine, and I know he could see tears starting to form in mine. I was furious. But I did eventually play and played quite a bit, in fact. I had learned my lesson. Coach was tough, but he was fair."

Like most anyone, when I think of Landry, I picture him patrolling the Cowboys sideline, neatly dressed in coat and tie and that ever-present fedora, hiding his progressively balding pate and shading his eyes from the sunlight pouring through the hole in the top of Texas Stadium. The arms were almost always crossed, and there rarely was a smile on his face.

There was something honorable, almost old-fashioned, in the manner in which Landry conducted himself as a man coaching a game played by grizzled, grown men with the hearts of exuberant boys. While Landry dressed for football games like most men usually dress for church—or at least how men used to dress to go to church in an era of pre-casual wear—there was never a sense that he thought of games as life-and-death struggles.

If he took losses hard, he never really showed it (and in his early years as Cowboys coach, he had plenty of opportunities to do just that). No throwing his hat. No tearing up of yardage markers. No grabbing/yanking of players' faceguards. No berating of officials. No gnashing of teeth. Those kinds of things were better left to the Vince Lombardis and Woody Hayeses of the sport. Then again, there were never any Landry moments of unbridled sideline joy, demonstrated by such acts as jumping into players' arms or racing over to the seats and high-fiving fans.

God forbid anyone ever try to dump a cooler of Gatorade on Landry's noggin in the waning moments of a championship-game victory. (Then again, by the time Gatorade showers had become an obligatory part of the game, Landry's Cowboys were no longer winning championship-caliber games.)

As a Giants fan growing up in upstate New York in the 1960s, seeing Landry and his Cowboys grew to be an annoying sight as the years went by and his Cowboys progressively improved to the point where they beat the Giants more often than not. In those days, a Cowboy victory was the last thing I wanted to see, especially when their opponent was my beloved New York Giants with the likes of Frank Gifford, Y.A. Tittle, Sam Huff, Tucker Frederickson, Joe Morrison, and Spider Lockhart.

Watching pro football in the 1960s, especially the Giants and occasionally the Cowboys—or anyone else for that matter—was an experience every bit as rich and memorable as games today, except they didn't have all the bells and whistles, or even the color picture, that today's telecasts, at times, trumpet to billions of viewers worldwide.

Growing up in upstate New York, NFL (and AFL) football on Sunday afternoons was every bit a part of the Northeast autumn fabric as burning piles of leaves, carving pumpkins, or sharpening ski edges and skate blades before the first fall of snow. There was no *Monday Night Football* in those days, no *Sunday Night Football,* no Super Bowls (until 1967), no Budweiser Bowls, no sideline reporters, no Jumbotrons, no super slo-mo, and Heidi had not yet made her NFL debut.

For Pete's sake, pro football was a Sunday afternoon-only phenomenon. If we were lucky, after the Giants played their 1:00 p.m. game on CBS, we would be treated to a second game that more than likely would feature either the Packers or the Rams. With any luck, Ray Scott was calling the game.

Games took less than three hours to play, allowing time for a brief postgame show before the second game kicked off at 4:00 p.m.

Those were the vintage days of Lombardi and Unitas, Landry and Brown, fourteen-game schedules and games played in snow or on ice without the benefit of on-field snowplows or indoor stadiums. It was true-blue football, limited camera angles and all, when a guy like Fran Tarkenton could scramble for days or Ernie Ladd could bodyslam a jitterbugging scatback without fear of a grievance being filed by the NFL Players Association.

That was the era in which Landry sharpened his pencil to become one of the greatest coaches the game has ever known, and he did it without the benefit of John Madden's advice, Al Davis's meddling, or reality TV.

To really get to know Landry, though, is to know a little of who and what he was before he became Dallas's own Rock of Gibraltar. First, he was a player, and a very good one at that. Yes, the sideline corporate CEO in suit and hat once wore shoulder pads and a helmet and took orders from coaches of his own. He was an All-Pro as a defensive back and as a punter. He would then become a player-coach and, finally, a coach, for several years forming half of the greatest coordinators' tandem in football history—he as defensive coordinator and none other than Vince Lombardi as offensive coordinator, plying their complementary trades under the supervision of Giants head coach Jim Lee Howell for much of the 1950s. In 1959 Lombardi would move on to become coach of the Green Bay Packers, followed a year later by Landry, who in 1960 was hired to coach the expansion Cowboys, a position he would hold until 1989.

The first time I met Coach Landry face-to-face was at the 1978 Super Bowl, when the Cowboys defeated the Denver Broncos to give Landry what would turn out to be his last Super Bowl triumph. I can remember to this day being so amused at how overjoyed he seemed to be. Don't know that I had ever seen him smile quite so emphatically, but he obviously had good reason to be happy. That was certainly a special season for the Cowboys, but even more so considering how quarterback Roger Staubach was just a year away from retiring, while Dorsett was a rookie running back quickly emerging as one of the best ball carriers in the league.

The Cowboys would never win a Super Bowl in the 1980s, instead experiencing a lot of frustration and the occasional heartbreak, such as when they dropped the 1980 NFC title game to Dick Vermeil and the Philadelphia Eagles, followed a year later by the memorable NFC Championship loss to the San Francisco 49ers. That was the game in which Joe Montana hit Dwight Clark running across the back of the end zone for a late touchdown pass that gave the 49ers a come-from-behind, 28–27 victory over Dallas.

A few days later, my dad called to tell me that I was on the cover of *Sports Illustrated*. He told me that I could be seen in the background in the end zone as Clark reached high over Dallas cornerback Everson Walls to make "The Catch."

Another vivid memory from that game was the plane ride from San Francisco home to Dallas with the team. It seemed to take forever. Almost silence the entire way, except for the music of my favorite group, Chicago, humming on the Sony Walkman I had just purchased at Fisherman's Wharf. Back then, the coaches sat in first class at the front of the plane, then the media, and, finally, the players toward the back. One of the passengers was former Miss America Phyllis George, from Denton, who was part of the NFL CBS broadcast team in those days. She was seated next to Cowboys general manager Tex Schramm. Coach Landry sat in front of him.

Further back in the plane, where I was sitting, quarterback Danny White was seated directly behind me, and I knew things were tough on Danny because he was following in the footsteps of the legendary Staubach. Understandably, White was devastated that his team had lost a one-point ballgame, and everybody knew how he felt. Staubach was even there with us on the flight, catching a ride home, and he came back and sat next to Danny in an attempt to console him. Roger tried to assure Danny that there would be other seasons, other opportunities, other chances to get to the big game.

On the other hand, I would look up at times and spot Coach Landry sitting toward the front, looking cool and calm while lost in a book he was reading. You'd never know it by seeing him at that moment, but here was a guy who just an hour or two earlier had seen his team lose in a really tough way, costing them a chance to play in another Super Bowl. As disappointed as he must have been, Landry never showed it. When we arrived in Dallas and as the players prepared to leave the plane, Landry calmly wished the players good luck in the off-season.

Just another day at the office.

Landry, however, was not an emotionless person. Take it from Bob Lilly, the Pro Football Hall of Fame Cowboys defensive tackle, who recalls the time when things weren't going so well for Landry and the Cowboys.

"It was Halloween of 1965, and we were in Pittsburgh to play the Steelers," Bob said. "We ended up losing that game for our fifth consecutive loss after starting the season 2–0. After the game, Coach Landry cleared the locker room, except for the players, and told us how proud he was of us all, despite the loss. He told us that he might not be there the next year, since we had won only twenty games in five and a half years. After he told us how proud he was of us, he broke down and cried."

Bob told me it was the only time he ever saw Landry cry, and I have no doubt that's true. In public, at least, Landry hardly ever laughed and he never cried, as far as I know. Certainly, that's the Landry my dad's mom, my grandmother, knew and loved. She was a huge Landry fan and would always ask me how "Ol' Stoneface" was. That's what my grandmother called him, and she would often tell me, "Tell him to smile." She was a real sports fan who really loved the coach for what he stood for, especially for his being a good Christian, embracing his faith as much as he proclaimed it.

My grandmother also was a big Danny White fan. To surprise her one time, I got Coach Landry and Danny to each autograph a poster of himself to give to her, and she was thrilled to get them. There she was, in her eighties, being so cool, hanging these poster-sized photos of both Landry and White on the back of her bedroom door. Is it any surprise that for so many years she was the talk of her neighborhood up in Canada?

Landry and the Cowboys had a knack for winning over members of my family, not just my grandmother. There's my sister, Debby, who for some odd reason had long been a Green Bay Packers and Lombardi fan. But all that changed in 1984, when I got tickets for my family to attend the Cowboys-Bills game in Buffalo the Sunday before Thanksgiving. They were excited because they got to sit in the Cowboys' section of the stadium and cheer for Dallas.

I had told Debby that, at the end of the game, she should take her son (my nephew), Scotty, around to where the buses were waiting to take the Cowboys back to the airport. Of course, I couldn't be there with her because of my broadcast duties. With any luck, they would get a chance to see some of the players.

When Debby and Scotty got there, she spotted Tex Schramm, told Scotty who it was, and he got Schramm's autograph. Debby would later tell me how Tex seemed so pleased because, as he told her, "Not many people outside of Texas ever ask me for my autograph. It's great to be recognized."

Just then, little Scotty spotted Coach Landry and mentioned it to his mom, and Debby just told him to be polite and to go for it, to ask Coach for his autograph. As Scotty approached the coach, who was walking swiftly past the fans and trying not to make eye contact with any of them (he must have been disappointed as well, as his Cowboys had just lost the game), Scotty stepped forward and said, "Coach Landry, can I please have your autograph?" Coach leaned over a bit and whispered down to Scotty, "Just keep walking with me."

Debby said, "He put his arm around Scotty and guided him in the direction he was walking." When they got to the bus, Coach leaned down to him and asked Scotty his name and then signed his program, and then he immediately stepped onto the bus. As excited as Scotty was in getting Coach Landry's autograph, it made an even greater impression on Debby, because he could have easily brushed off Scotty as he hurried to the bus. Until the day she died of breast cancer, there wasn't a bigger Cowboys fan around than Debby. This was all because of Coach Landry. He took the time to make a difference and put a smile on the faces of a little boy and his mom. Those are the little things that set Coach Landry apart.

There are so many things about Coach Landry worth remembering for a lifetime, and the memories come in all shapes and sizes. For one thing, he was not always the obsessively stoic, stone-faced coach we saw in public. Landry had a terrific dry sense of humor, even humor of the self-deprecating sort. Like the time in 1982, when there was an NFL strike, and I got hold of the outtakes from an American Express television commercial the coach had done with a couple of players from the Washington Redskins. There was some really funny, goofy stuff in there, and when I interviewed him about it, he just loved it. As a matter of fact, we won an award from the Associated Press for that feature we did on Coach Landry and the American Express commercial.

There also was the time that place-kicker Rafael Septien hired a woman in a short, frilly skirt to surprise Coach Landry on his birthday in the middle of a team meeting. We had been tipped off to it at NBC 5, and I showed up with a camera crew and shot it. This woman got Coach Landry to put on a dunce cap and start blowing a party-favor horn as the players sang "Happy Birthday." Landry was a good sport about the whole thing.

As it was all winding down, Coach Landry spotted me with the camera crew and motioned for me to come over. When I got over to him, he leaned over to me and whispered, "Please don't show that on television. This is a team meeting, and what happens in here is family and stays here." It's kind of like the TV commercial that says, "What happens in Vegas stays in Vegas." I assured him no one would ever see it, and while I've held on to that tape for years, I've never shown it to anyone. But it really is hilarious. It also shows a real human side to Tom Landry that few have ever seen.

Another example of his great wit comes from a story told to me by veteran news writer and author Bob St. John, who also was one of Coach Landry's longtime acquaintances. Bob tells the story of a trip the Cowboys took to Yankee Stadium in 1970 to play the Giants. The police got a report that there was a bomb in the press box, but the game went on, and there was no explosion. During the postgame interviews, Landry was asked what he would have done if a bomb had gone off in the press box and blown up all the writers. As Bob tells it, the coach, expressionless, paused for a second and then said, "I suppose we would have observed thirty seconds of silent prayer, then continued to play with enthusiasm and vigor." Then Coach Landry broke into the widest smile anyone had ever seen from him. Once again, that was Tom Landry—always in control.

That bomb scare reminds me of another story involving a threat, and this time it directly involved Landry. It was at a Monday night game in Anaheim between the Cowboys and the Rams, and it was an incident that showed Coach's great courage, commitment, and faith. Larry Wansley, a former FBI agent who had been hired by the Cowboys as director of security, would later tell me that stadium officials had received an anonymous call that there was a sniper in the stadium and Landry's life had been threatened. Larry told the coach of the phoned-in threat and immediately ushered him back into the locker room.

Without offering any details, Coach Landry had told Danny White, who was injured at the time, to call the plays with Steve Pelleur at quarterback in his absence. Danny had no idea what was going on, nor did the national TV audience, nor, at first, did many of us in the press box. But despite suggestions that he remain off the field during the game, Coach said no. He put on a bulletproof vest under his shirt and coat, then returned to the field and coached. As it turned out, there apparently never was a sniper in the stadium, and the Cowboys won the game. Once again, that was Coach Landry for you: cool, calm, and collected.

The only time I saw him get at all flustered, much to the amusement of the media, was in 1984 during a function at the Hyatt Regency. It was a welcome-home, kickoff luncheon for the Cowboys, at which I was to be the master of ceremonies. Prior to the luncheon, there would be a media news conference, at which time Coach Landry would announce who his starting quarterback would be for the season opener. Up until then, there had been some debate as to whether it would be Danny White or Gary Hogeboom.

Now, keep in mind that Coach would occasionally mispronounce or forget a name, as he was prone to do time and again in butchering the pronunciation of Hogeboom's name. This time, he took it to another level. When it came time to announce his decision, Coach Landry uttered, "I've decided my starting quarterback will be—Phil Pozderac."

Well, Pozderac was the offensive left tackle out of Notre Dame, and he was nowhere to be found on the quarterback depth chart. Where that came from, nobody knew. Danny was Coach's guy, but there still was such controversy about benching him in favor of Hogeboom, that apparently the stress of wrestling with the decision got to Landry. It was the rarest of occasions when he wasn't in total control, showing calm and cool with the situation, although the one plus that came out of it was for Pozderac—it was the most press he got all season. It also was the closest he ever came to playing quarterback for the Dallas Cowboys.

One of my favorite Landry stories happened years earlier during a time-out in a game, when Staubach came to the sideline to get a play from Landry. "I waited forever for Coach to make a decision as he just gazed through the hole in the stadium roof for the longest time," Staubach said. "Finally, he lowered his gaze, looked over at me, and told me what play to run. As I started running back onto the field, I said to him, 'Coach, I always wondered where you got those plays.' I know he heard me, but he never made a move, even though all the coaches around him were laughing."

So much can be learned about a man and what kind of father he is, simply by getting to know his son. The same can be said for a coach and the respect he gets from his players. For example, "Mr. Cowboy," Bob Lilly. I have never, I mean never, heard Bob give a speech or address a group without giving testimony to the respect he had for and the resolve he took from Coach Landry. He just idolizes the man. The simple influence of Landry changed Lilly's life. And now, Bob continues to do much the same, speaking to companies and youth groups around the country about the importance of making the right choices in life. Another pupil of Landry's was Hall of Fame lineman Rayfield Wright, who says he'll always remember the words of Coach in a farewell to his players, "The way you react to adversity is the key to success. Adversity will defeat losers while inspiring winners." For a young man who was raised by his grandmother in a fatherless home, Rayfield Wright, like so many others, looked upon Tom Landry as more than just a football coach. He was a teacher, a mentor, an influence, and yes, even a father of sorts. "I watched how he did things and learned from him," said Rayfield, "There wasn't a written rule that said we had to wear a suit and tie while traveling to road games. We just knew it was right because Coach Landry did it. There was no rule about who deplaned or got off the bus first, yet we always waited for Coach and Mrs. Landry to leave ahead of us, simply out of respect. And when I think of the gentle manner in which he treated his wife, Alicia, it was the first time that many players in that genre had ever been exposed to such graciousness. It was a tremendous, unspoken lesson to us all." That was Coach Landry, again, leading by example, without saying a thing.

Knowing the impact that Coach Landry had on so many of his players, I often wondered to what extent the "Big Cat" was influenced in making one of the most compassionate, heart-warming decisions of his life. The year was 1973. Rayfield was taping an off-season TV commercial for a foster parent group. "As the cameras were about to roll," said Wright, "a woman approached me and gently cradled two babies in my arms. As I studied their beautiful faces, my eyes immediately focused on their eyes. They literally captured your soul and spoke to your heart with a divine innocence. Not only did I see their eyes, I saw their souls and felt their spirits. As I finished taping, I found it hard to give the babies back. I asked the woman if they were looking for parents or needed a home. She said, 'yes,' to which I answered, 'I'd like to be their father.' My wife and I had no children, so we adopted these blessings from God. Now twenty-three years later, our son is a recent graduate of SMU with a master's degree in business administration. My daughter majored in biochemical engineering at Harvard."

There was one man who set the tone and the culture for America's Team for twenty-nine years, and that man was Tom Landry. In some ways, it is a tone and culture that exists with the Cowboys to this day, although much has changed too. It was a sad day when Coach Landry was relieved of his duties, although I knew it was coming because of the inside source we had at NBC 5.

When we broke the story that Thursday night, February 23, 1989, that Jerry Jones was going to buy the Cowboys from Bum Bright, I couldn't help but feel some concern for the Schramm family as well as for Tom and Alicia Landry and their family. The Cowboys had been their public life for almost thirty years. On the other hand, Dallas was coming off a 3–13 season and the franchise was about ten years removed from its last Super Bowl appearance.

Many fans were infuriated with the legendary coach, and the media was second-guessing almost his every move (and non-move). This was not the Cowboys team football fans had come to take for granted, so, while the timing was abrupt, it might have been the best thing for all concerned. Jones certainly had every right to make a break with the past and start rebuilding a franchise his way, and it was as good a time as any for Landry to get away from the public abuse laid on him for his team's poor performance. Jones would later say that it was Bright, not he, who had left Landry and Schramm out in the cold, upset that the Cowboys were never competitive during his ownership reign. Jones wanted his own brain trust—with him included, obviously—running the team, and that would not have been possible with Landry and Schramm.

By sending Landry packing in this manner, Jones was actually doing a favor for the by-now beleaguered coach. He turned Landry into an immediate martyr and a sympathetic character, giving Cowboys fans an opportunity to turn their anger into appreciation for this icon, who had helped build "America's Team" from scratch. All the angst from the past few seasons had been suddenly lifted from everyone's shoulders, and again Landry could be celebrated in the manner that he deserved.

More than anything else, Landry would be remembered for the character, dignity, and grace he brought to the job. The images were emblazoned on our collective consciousness: the coat and tie, the trademark fedora, the crossed arms, the rolled-up game plan, the stone face, and the stoic demeanor. At a city-wide parade in Dallas to honor him, hundreds of thousands turned out to salute Tom and Alicia. It was a huge celebration. Television stations around the state preempted their programming to show the event live. Soon, schools, highways, and athletic fields would be named in his honor. There was his induction into the Pro Football Hall of Fame, eventually to be followed by his induction into the Cowboys Ring of Honor after an initial reluctance to be so honored by the Jones administration.

In 1993 I approached Coach Landry about creating the Tom Landry Award for Excellence with Tiffany and Company. Both parties agreed, and it was decreed that the award would be given to those who make a difference in the world of children in need. I'll never forget how humbled I was a few years later, when Coach called me up and said, "I want you to have the award this year, and you can't say no. You deserve it." As you can imagine, I was honored to receive anything with Tom Landry's name attached to it.

More and more during his retirement, our friendship flourished, and my respect for the man blossomed. After one of his daughters, Lisa, lost her battle to cancer, his other daughter, Kitty, asked me to become a member of the board of the Lisa Landry Childress Foundation. Of course, I accepted, and it was not long after that that Coach had his own battle to deal with: he had been diagnosed with leukemia. Coach Landry would ultimately pass away on a February 12 (2000), the birthday of Abraham Lincoln, another great man of honor, honesty, and humility.

For someone who has had the opportunity to cover so many sporting events, meet so many gifted sports figures, and travel to so many exciting locations, I really don't have that many keepsakes to show for it. You would think I had hundreds, but I don't. Dozens perhaps. Of the few that really have personal meaning to me, and which I've kept, two are related to Landry, excluding the cherished award that bears his name: one is a framed photo of Landry and me on the sidelines where I was playing in a flag football game for charity at Texas Stadium; the other is an autographed fedora of his that I bought at a charity auction. I put both items in a shadowbox that hangs in my study, and it has become quite a conversation piece when people see it. To me, though, it's much more than that.

As a journalist, you always strive to get the facts correct, to be fair and nonpartisan in your reporting, and to never become part of the story that you're covering. However, that last part was a tough go on that day in February 2000, when we paid our last respects to Tom Landry at his funeral. Standing in front of the church, you could see scores of former players and coaches, many of whom went on to become head coaches themselves, such as Mike Ditka, John Mackovic, Dan Reeves, Dick Nolan, Neil Armstrong, and Gene Stallings, among others. That speaks to the impact Coach Landry had on so many. Also present were former competitive adversaries, such as Kansas City Chiefs owner Lamar Hunt, who revered Coach Landry for his intelligence, innovation, and integrity. Hunt, himself, is similar in that regard, in the balanced and character-driven way he has lived his own life. Like Landry, Lamar is a man of monumental stature and grace and has always been a visionary.

Tom Landry was a rock, a constant. He also was a man of great faith, a devout Christian who steadily walked the tightrope between proclaiming his faith and cramming it down people's throats. It should surprise no one that he had such an affinity for the Fellowship of Christian Athletes.

During the 1980s and into the 1990s, I often served as the emcee for the Cotton Bowl Breakfast sponsored each year by the FCA. Because of his involvement as a member of the national board and as a longtime spokesman of FCA, Coach Landry would regularly deliver the invocation. This provided me an additional opportunity to get to know Tom Landry the person as well as the coach, and I must admit that he's one of the reasons I've stayed involved as a member of the North Texas Board of FCA for twenty-five years. The FCA golf tournament in Dallas that bears Landry's name continues to be one of the most popular and profitable charity events in Texas, while "Mr. Cowboy" and I are proud to have just completed our twenty-fifth year of the Bob Lilly/Scott Murray FCA Golf Tournament, benefiting the Summer Huddle Programs in Fort Worth and north Texas. Again, our long-term commitment's due in great part to Coach Landry.

Over time, my relationship with Coach and his family grew stronger and became more than just football coach and sports journalist. I was again reminded of that special friendship early in 2006, when I received a note from Coach's widow, Alicia (with whom I have kept in touch), asking me to join with other special friends of the family's at a memorial service at the Texas State Cemetery in Austin. There was going to be a dedication of a large, beautiful, engraved, silver-blue granite monument that was to be unveiled in honor of Coach Landry. It would sit among the other prominent monuments in the cemetary honoring former governors and other famous Texans.

It was a service attended by about a hundred people. Tom Jr., Kitty, and Alicia were all there, of course. Also present were Texas governor Rick Perry and his wife, Anita, as well as Staubach, Lilly, Charlie Waters, Grant Teaff, Darrell Royal, and others. It was an impressive group. We gathered in the cemetery for a short service, then proceeded to the Austin Club for an intimate gathering. It was friends. It was fellowship. It was family. It was faith. All gathered together, remembering one man. Incredible.

Even in death, people always find time for Coach—and always will. That was and is the impact and influence of Tom Landry.

JOHNNY RUTHERFORD

CHARITY

*You make a living by what you get,
you make a life by what you give.*

—Winston Churchill

A uto racing must have been in my genes. Engineering sure was, and as we all know, engineering is a key component of auto racing. My dad was an engineer, so I had plenty of help at home when it came to designing one of those little, scaled-down race cars you use to compete with in the Cub Scouts Racing Derby.

Thanks to Dad's suggestion to put some lead in the bottom of my car to help weigh it down and make it faster, I finished second overall out of one hundred Scouts my first year. His engineering acumen allowed me to win the following year against a field twice as big as it was the first time around.

Working together on those model-like race cars in my dad's shop were precious times, even if I didn't fully appreciate them at the time. I can still smell the paint and feel the shavings that fell while fashioning the little cars via some painstaking handiwork. Dad always seemed to know exactly what he was doing. The thing that caught my eye the most were his hands and his fingers, how steady they were and precise in their workmanship. Getting the car just right was as much a challenge for him as it was a goal of mine. In all respects, I always felt total security knowing that Dad had things in his hands. For a boy, there is no greater source of security than a dad who spends time with him, lending that emotional support as well.

It's funny what people will remember over the years—the images, the scents, even the sounds. I remember building model cars with my father vividly even though minutes raced by without conversation while we focused on certain aspects of the car-construction process. Ours was a silence of contentment and focus as we were doing what we loved. It was always about more than just the car itself to me; it was the twinkle in Dad's eyes—yes, there was a twinkle, as it was obvious he found great relaxation in those times he spent with me working on the little race cars. The finished product was always exciting, a source of deep satisfaction. But even more priceless was the quiet bonding that took place between us, much like when we worked together for hours on my model train layout.

Aside from my dad's love of hockey, which was in his genes, with his being from Canada, it might be somewhat of a surprise to know that auto racing was his second love. And that rubbed off on me, from an early age, and keep in mind that was long before NASCAR became anything close to what it is now. The proof is on the shelving: both of those cars from my Cub Scout days are on a bookshelf in my study—one is black with yellow stripes and the other blue with white stripes. Yet there is plenty of other auto racing memorabilia around to keep them company.

From as far back as I can remember, whenever my family and I went to an amusement park, the first stop, at least for me, was any attraction on wheels. Get me in one of those motorized cars or go-carts, buckle me in, and get out of the way.

Dad would often talk about the Formula One circuit in Great Britain, as well as Watkins Glen—just eighty miles away for us—and the great drivers of his day. Sterling Moss. John Surtess. Phil Hill. I remember going to Watkins Glen as a kid and seeing Jim Clark win there back-to-back in 1966 and 1967. He also was a two-time world champion and truly a favorite driver of mine, which made it hurt all the more when he was killed in a crash in 1968. Clark was only thirty-two at the time, and I felt his death as though I'd lost a part of the family. It was then that I learned about and came to respect the fine line between life and death that exists in auto racing.

Elsewhere in this book I have shared some of my daydreams—call them Walter Mitty moments—that define my love for sports. Like many sports fans, they include hitting a home run to win the World Series for the Yankees, and leading my football team on a winning touchdown drive in the closing minutes. But if you really want to get a goose-bumps rise out of me, bring up the topic of auto racing and ask me if I've ever thought about handling the wheel of a high-powered race car with the pedal to the metal. Most people who know me still don't realize that, to this day, if I could choose any profession other than the one I have dearly enjoyed, it would be to be a Formula One race car driver. For starters, there would be the chance to travel throughout Europe, Asia, and South America. Very appealing.

Driving a race car at well over two hundred miles an hour on a racetrack is worlds removed from laying rubber with Dad's '68 Olds 442 on some lonely stretch of State Highway 31 at two in the morning, the speedometer's needle pinned to the right (well, almost). Race cars, whether they be the Indy variety, NASCAR, Formula One, or even your souped-up, funny car at the local drag strip, are finely tuned machines that require the touch of a surgeon, the nerves of an air traffic controller, and the will of a special forces grunt pinned down in a foxhole under a barrage of fire from dozens of hostiles.

It's hammering along on a twisting track at more than two hundred miles an hour, making split-second decisions, one after another, any of which could mean instant death if it's wrong. All this while being bumped, drafted, sideswiped, passed, and pursued by a bunch of other professional drivers with about as much concern for your welfare as you have for that roach that just ended up on your plate at the corner meat-and-three.

Ah, yes, the drivers—certainly a different breed.

Another favorite of Dad's was Bruce McLaren. What a thrill getting to see him drive at Watkins Glen. Dad would always talk about McLaren and his great talent, and yet, like Clark, he also died young, killed racing while testing tires. In telling me about McLaren's death, Dad passed along parts of a McLaren quote he had once heard about taking advantage of the moment and not letting any grass grow under your feet. Stay focused. Keep motivated. Always be moving forward and experiencing all the positive things that life has to offer.

Life is measured in achievement, not in years alone. Good stuff, and definitely words to live by.

I finally got a chance to feed my need for speed when Dad relented and let our next-door neighbor, who happened to be an official at Watkins Glen, take me around the track at the Glen in his jaguar at a pretty good clip. What a rush that was.

When we weren't at the Glen, from the time I was ten or eleven, Sundays after church in the summer months were spent at the "Hill Climb," across the lake from our summer cottage. Dad and I would watch motorcyclists simply defy gravity by racing straight up these incredibly steep, high hills. You never got tired of watching.

As I look back, it seems that just about anything with wheels and a motor in it was enough to entertain us. And, yet, what really put it all over the top was simply getting to do it with my dad.

It was in 1980 that I finally got a real taste of racing, and that was after I moved from Washington, D.C. to Texas. That was the year that I met Johnny Rutherford, who had just won his third Indy 500. He was my first television interview in Texas at my new sports anchor position, and he made a lasting impression. Obviously.

Talk about making my day. As soon as I finished the interview, I found a pay phone in the Holiday Inn in Fort Worth, where I had done the interview, and immediately called my dad to tell him with whom I had just spoken. He was thrilled and wanted to hear all about it, sharing in the moment and reliving J.R.'s win less than two months earlier at Indianapolis.

Rutherford won his three Indy 500s in 1974, 1976, and 1980, putting him in a truly elite class of Indy drivers. He is one of only seven drivers who have officially won at least three Indy 500s, and when you see the list of peers in his group, you can understand how great a driver he was. Other three-time winners include Louis Meyer, Wilbur Shaw, A. J. Foyt, Al Unser, Bobby Unser, and Rick Mears.

In a sense, though, you could say that Rutherford has flown under the radar just a bit, never achieving the kind of superstar cult status that the likes of Shaw, Foyt, and the two Unsers did. The irony there is that Rutherford has done some nifty high flying of his own, having piloted, as a hobby, the P-51 Mustang fighter plane that gained notoriety during World War II. Rutherford's dad was an aviator with a passion for his hobby, auto racing, and Johnny was just the other way around.

The younger Rutherford saw his first race in person at a quarter-mile dirt track when he was nine years old. His love for racing took hold while he was in high school and a member of a hot rod club. After seeing a race at Devil's Bowl Speedway in Dallas, he got his buddies to help him build a car, and eventually, in 1959, an auto racing career was born when he started out driving Modifieds at Devil's Bowl. He raced his first Indy car in 1962, then three years later, in 1965, he won the United States Auto Club's sprint championship. His first Indy-car victory came that same year, when he won a 250-miler in Atlanta.

Glossing over the many highlights of Rutherford's racing career doesn't really do him justice, though. There has been heartbreak as well, such as the time in 1966 when he broke both arms when he crashed in a sprint-car event, forcing him to miss Indy that year. Two years later, he suffered bad hand burns in a wreck at Phoenix.

As a footnote to his great racing career, Rutherford in his early days of racing tried his hand at Winston Cup racing. In fact he won the first such event he ever started, a hundred-mile qualifier for the 1963 Daytona 500. In those days, such qualifier events counted as official races.

It wasn't until 1976 that Johnny would get his legendary CB handle as "Lone Star J.R.," a nickname which has stayed with him ever since, making him perhaps the second-most-famous J.R. found in Texas, and certainly No. 1 if you don't count fictional TV characters.

Living and working in Texas gave me plenty of opportunities to meet a good number of professionals in the auto racing industry, from owners, to drivers, to pit crews. And I never turned down a chance to get behind the wheel as a driver in celebrity/charity races at area tracks and speedways. That was heaven.

Things got more interesting in 1984, when a group of investors announced they were going to bring the Formula One circuit to Dallas, specifically at and around Fair Park in south Dallas, where the Cotton Bowl resides. The station sent me to Montreal to cover the Canadian Grand Prix, part of the Formula One circuit. This was our chance to acquaint our viewers with the drivers and the sport, during which time I did a TV segment with Hall of Famer Jackie Stewart. I kept Dad abreast of all my goings-on, especially when I went to Montreal and met the likes of Stewart, because Dad was so familiar with Montreal—my folks had honeymooned there—and because now I was talking to these guys on a different level.

Another of my interview subjects that week in Montreal was Austria's Niki Lauda, who had won the Canadian Grand Prix. Lauda was the famous driver whose face had been scarred and disfigured from a fire in his car during a race in Germany in 1976, and, again, it was a visible reminder of how dangerous the sport can be.

As the Dallas race approached, the organizers must have been reading my thoughts, because they decided to schedule a celebrity race. The only prerequisite was that if you wanted to compete, you had to attend a driving school at the Laguna Seca track in Monterey, California. They didn't have to strong-arm me to do it—I jumped at the chance.

The racing school was a great experience. Our class of seven got to meet actor-driver-owner Paul Newman as well as Rick Mears, who had just won that year's Indy 500. We drove from morning till night, which explains why I was rarin' to go by the time we got back to Texas, where I drove in a field comprised mostly of Hollywood celebs, including a number of cast members from the TV show *Dallas*.

I invited my folks to come down and watch the race, which turned out to be a great time. Rutherford and I cohosted an hour-long TV special we put together to preview the race, and this gave my dad a chance to meet Johnny for the first time. It's moments like that that provided the big payoff for me, more so for what it meant to my dad than what it meant to me.

It wasn't just because Rutherford was a famous name that my dad was so psyched to be around him; it was because he knew enough about Rutherford to know what a considerate guy he was. My dad already knew Rutherford as someone who not only showed appreciation for his fans but who gave back to the sport and showed incredible generosity to so many worthy causes. He was, and is, a charitable man, both with his time and his finances, willing to share of himself for the betterment of others.

I would get to know Johnny a lot better as the years passed. I suppose it didn't hurt his knowing how much of a racing aficionado I was, who could not only report the stories but walk the walk, or at least talk it. As time passed, Johnny and I would often end up at the same charity functions together, allowing Carole and me a chance to get to know Johnny and his wonderful wife, Betty, a little better.

Johnny and Betty actually met at Indy in the early 1960s when he first started racing there, and she was a nurse at the infield hospital—at one point having to tend to the young driver. Betty herself has long been an organizer of charity events, and she's a real dynamo at it. They really are an accomplished couple—and a lot of fun to be around.

One of the many enterprising things Betty did was starting the Indy Racing Wives charity organization in 1981, doing so after learning that some of the NASCAR wives were doing something similar for hospitalized children. And when Texas Motor Speedway was built in 1996, Betty was asked to be the founding president of the Speedway Children's Charity Board in Texas. She thoughtfully asked me to be on the board of trustees, a position I am honored to hold to this day. In the first nine years, we have raised more than $3 million.

Along with the Speedway came my introduction to Legends Car Racing. The cars are small replicas of those used in the 1934–40 era, and I became the proud owner of a black 1940 Ford Coupe. I ate it up so much that I went ahead and started my own annual charity race at the Speedway with the assistance of well-known celebrities—athletes, singers, TV personalities, corporate leaders, politicians, et al.

Johnny normally served as my honorary chair, but he did it in a hands-on way that delighted those who came to watch, taking some time to get out to work the crowd and work some of his magic, signing autographs, posing for pictures, probably kissing a few babies, for all I know. Anything to help the cause. On top of that, I can't count the number of times Johnny and Betty have donated Indy 500 passes, garage and pit passes, and VIP suite seats to assist any number of charities. The Rutherfords just enjoy making a difference in the lives of folks who need a helping hand.

Johnny remains active in the Indy Racing League, driving the pace car at all of the sanctioned IRL races during the racing season. He has also served as the driving instructor for the likes of Colin Powell, Jay Leno, Morgan Freeman, Jim Caviezel, and Lance Armstrong—celebrities who have driven the honorary pace car at the famed brickyard during the Indianapolis 500.

J.R. loves telling stories about the experience. Like the day he had Freeman (who played the part of God in *Bruce Almighty*) and Caviezel (who played the part of Jesus in *The Passion of the Christ*) on the track together. When they arrived back in the pits after completing their practice laps, one very excited motor/movie buff ran over to Johnny in awe and exclaimed, "Do you realize you just taught God and Jesus to drive at Indianapolis?"

The drivers of today have obviously taken a cue or two from J.R.'s benevolent lead when it comes to charitable involvement. As a celebrity participant in this year's Sam Hornish Jr. Charity Bowling Tournament, I saw firsthand how committed and supportive Sam (this year's Indy 500 Champion), his always effervescent teammate Helio Castroneves, and fellow

IRL drivers are by taking time and giving back to boys and girls in need, as they raised thousands for the Speedway Children's Charities, while putting smiles on the faces of hundreds of race fans. A few of them even pulled out their own checkbooks. And, to no one's surprise, "Lone Star J.R." was right there, once again lending his support to a charitable cause.

Mom and Dad would try to come to Texas twice a year to visit us and see their grandchildren, Doug and Stephanie. Whenever possible, we'd work their trip around a Cowboys game, a Stars game, or an auto-racing event. My dad loved the hockey and auto racing, while my mom had a place in her heart for the Cowboys. Something for everyone. It afforded us the opportunity each visit to share something we had shared while I was growing up, except we were now living it instead of just talking about it.

It gets even better. Two years ago in a raffle, I won a week's stay in the condos at the Speedway during the week of the Indy race. I asked my parents to come down and join us in this huge, two-bedroom condo. Every morning at dawn we would wake up to the high-pitched squeal of those Indy car engines. Talk about an alarm clock! We could walk ten steps from the bedroom and overlook the whole track, cars whizzing by at about 215 miles per hour. My dad absolutely loved it. On race day, we fixed him up with some VIP passes to visit the pits and garage area, I was also able to purchase a ride for Dad in the parade lap with Michael Andretti, allowing him to ride around the track as the crowds screamed and waved. It was an experience of a lifetime for my dad and a memorable opportunity for me to share it with him.

There is something about the whole motor-racing community that reeks of family. And that family has proven to be most charitable over the years. Whether it's the Rutherfords and the Indy Racing League or NASCAR and families like the Pettys, time and time again they have proven to be on the fast track when it comes to being generous, benevolent, giving people. Willing to take parts of their lives (whether it's their time, talent, or money) to make a difference in someone else's life. They all take the checkered flag when it comes to charity. That's why you'll always find guys like Johnny Rutherford in Victory Lane.

XXII

CAL
RIPKEN JR.

DURABILITY

Patience and perseverance have a magical effect before which difficulties disappear and obstacles vanish.

—John Quincy Adams

L ong before Cal Ripken Jr. had played in his 2,632nd consecutive baseball game as a major leaguer, he was a favorite among us Murrays. Cal, his dad, my dad, and I—unbeknownst to the Ripkens, of course—go back a long way, in fact years before Cal Jr. had even made it to the major leagues.

Considering the respective, and respectful, father-son relationships here, it's also poetic justice of sorts that baseball's two greatest ironmen are bound together in the pages of this book, in large part in both cases because of how my dad held them in such high regard. Anyone with Dad's stamp of approval got similar treatment from me.

Even without their respective consecutive-games-played marks, Lou Gehrig and Ripken both lived up to the highest standards that go with being a genuine sports role model as well as one of the greatest players of their respective eras.

An argument could be made that Ripken, who retired in 2001, was overshadowed by his record mark of 2,632 consecutive games played. Speak his name, and the first thing that comes to mind is "The Streak." You might say he was underrated, never fully appreciated for the great overall player and team leader he was because so much of what he was in the public eye was defined by "The Streak." When he finally took himself out of the lineup late in the 1998 season, he had beaten Gehrig's record streak by 502 games. Yet, there still was a sense that he might have hurt himself in the long run, subjecting himself to years of wear and tear, when other players typically take five to ten games off in a season for some much needed rest and recharging.

Before we dig too deep into the denouement of Ripken's career, let's go back to the beginning. Better yet, let's go back to before the beginning, and that takes us back to the Rochester, New York area, where I grew up. So did Cal Jr. to some degree. In both Cal's case and mine, we were there because of our fathers—Cal Jr. because his dad worked for the Baltimore Orioles' Triple-A club in Rochester, and I because my dad and mom had moved there so my dad could pursue his career in engineering.

Ripken sure made a difference for millions of admirers, more so for his sportsmanship and humility than just for his playing records punctuated by his durability. I guess you could say he was a chip off the old block, because long before there was a Cal Jr. and baseball had its new Ironman, there was Cal Sr. That's the Cal Ripken I grew up knowing, the one who managed the Orioles' Rochester Red Wings. I can remember my dad talking about Cal Sr. with a lot of admiration. Dad liked him because he was a no-nonsense guy who lived in a black-and-white world, just like he did.

Cal Sr. and my dad were two of a mind: fair, and not big fans of excuses. They both felt that people should be accountable for what they did as well as what they stood for. Very little gray. No doubt that same attitude rubbed off on Cal Jr., who shared his dad's convictions and yet did it with modesty and graciousness. Cal Jr. was one of the good guys in sports, always willing to give time to the media for an umpteenth interview and always aware of his status as a role model on and off the field. I don't remember his ever doing anything to shoot himself in the foot in the public eye. Class act all around.

When I signed a contract with NBC and went to work in Washington, D.C., I got to cover the Orioles because D.C. didn't have a baseball team at the time. I met Junior at a charity basketball game we all played in at a local high school, and he was good. It's no wonder he has a basketball court in his house to this day.

As good an athlete as he was, though, the most striking thing about Ripken is how down to earth he is. He's about as unpretentious as they get. Very balanced and even-keeled. He finally went up to the majors in the early

'80s, and that's where he would stay for some twenty years without ever getting sent to the minors or traded to another team—a show of stability rarely seen in sports anymore.

I remember his telling me about how he hit a home run in his first major league at-bat, only to quickly go into a major slump. He was afraid he was going to be sent down, but as short-tempered as manager Earl Weaver was, he simply called Ripken into his office and told him to relax and not worry, that he wasn't going anywhere. Ripken has never forgotten that vote of confidence from Weaver and said it made a huge difference in his maturation process.

I have always liked the way he handled himself. There were no extreme highs or extreme lows with him. When Cal passed Gehrig's record in 1995, my father was practically beside himself, because he knew as well as anyone that there was no one better suited to carry that mantle than Ripken.

Even as Ripken's career was winding down and his output was dwindling, he still was kind enough to do a couple of lengthy interviews with me in his final years. After his retirement, I went to Aberdeen—the Baltimore suburb where he is from—and did a one-hour television show focused on Ripken. It was done at his old high school (even though it's a new building) in front of an appreciative audience of a thousand people. It was a one-on-one interview, and we talked about baseball, his teammates, family, friends, and life. For the most part, he kept his composure, only to be emotionally overcome for a moment when talking about his dad, Cal Sr., and his own son. It was great seeing the real Cal, a side of him that we often don't get a chance to see.

After we finished taping, Cal hung around for quite a while to mix and mingle with the crowd, and it was clear that he was enjoying himself.

That said, a closer scrutiny of Ripken's career is in order to better appreciate what he accomplished. It is true that his final career batting average of .276, while respectable, falls somewhat below the norm for Hall of Fame–caliber players. Keep in mind, though, that by the time Mickey Mantle and Willie

Mays retired, their career batting averages had dipped to .298 and .302, respectively. So when you put Ripken next to two of the greatest all-around players of the last fifty years, his .276 average holds up fairly well, especially when one considers his willingness to avoid days off so as to help his team.

Now, let's look at the glass as half full. In fourteen of his twenty-one seasons, Ripken hit twenty or more home runs. He also knocked in ninety or more runs eight times. He won two American League Most Valuable Player awards, was 1982 AL Rookie of the Year, set a record for shortstops in 1990 when he committed only three errors, and in 1983 he helped lead the Baltimore Orioles to the World Series title.

His long-term durability and prowess were reflected not only in his streak and his having played 3,001 games but in the fact that he hit 431 career home runs and collected 3,184 hits total. Only one other American Leaguer has ever reached both the 3,000 mark for career hits and 400 homers, and that player is Boston Red Sox Hall of Famer Carl Yastrzemski. That's fast company.

There are some interesting aspects of Ripken's games-played streak that go beyond the final number itself. There were the close calls to ending the streak prematurely, such as when he twisted his right ankle while legging out a double against the Milwaukee Brewers on September 11, 1992, or when he twisted his right knee when his spikes got caught on the infield turf during an Orioles-Mariners brawl on June 6, 1996. Although the knee was swollen and painful the next day, Ripken managed to play the game. He was even out there before the game for infield practice. "It was the closest I've come to not playing," Ripken would later admit.

Another streak breaker narrowly averted was the players' strike that started on August 12, 1994, just eleven days after Ripken had played in his two thousandth consecutive game. In September the owners canceled the remainder of the 1994 season, and by the next March there were rumors that the owners would start the 1995 season by fielding teams consisting of replacement players. Those games would have counted as official games played, meaning that

Ripken's streak would have been stopped one game into the season if he didn't play. Had it come to that, it turns out, Ripken announced that he would honor the players' strike and not cross the picket line, even if it meant breaking his streak less than a season short of catching Gehrig.

While all this was going on, Orioles owner Peter Angelos announced that if it actually came to "scabs" playing in place of the "real" players, he would not allow it, out of respect for Ripken and his streak. The strike was soon settled, however, and the 1995 season eventually was played with the real players in uniform and taking the field. Ripken's streak was still intact.

Ripken finally caught Gehrig at 2,130 consecutive games on September 5, 1995, at Camden Yards, receiving a five-minute ovation when the game became official in the bottom of the fifth inning. For good measure, he hit a home run as the Orioles defeated the California Angels, 8–0. He also homered the next night in a 4–2 victory over the Angels, marking his 2,131st straight game played, moving him past Gehrig once and for all. This time he got a twenty-two-minute ovation, and he took a victory lap around the field.

Beyond that, he would go on to play more than three full seasons' worth of games before finally taking himself out of the lineup on September 20, 1998, before the Orioles' last home game of the season. His Ironman days were over. The following April, he went where he had never gone before—onto the disabled list, not just once but twice. Ripken would end up playing in only eighty-six games in 1999. Ironically, he would end up batting .340 that season, which would have been a career high had he accumulated enough official at-bats.

Ripken would get one last hurrah in 2000, when he joined the elite club of those with three thousand career hits. Otherwise his last two seasons showed he was obviously winding down, finishing 2000 with a .256 batting average, playing only eighty-three games after missing much of two seasons while on the DL. He was healthier in 2001, but a late-season slump left his average at .239, the lowest of his distinguished career. One saving grace was his making his record seventeenth start in the All-Star Game while extending his appearance string in All-Star Games to nineteen. He did hit a homer in the game to earn his second All-Star MVP Award.

At his Camden Yards retirement ceremony in October 2001, after the Orioles' season was over, Ripken told a capacity crowd, "One question I've been repeatedly asked these last few weeks is how do I want to be remembered. My answer is simple: To be remembered at all is pretty special. I might also add, that if I am remembered, I hope it's because by living my dream, I was able to make a difference."

To give you an idea of what I think of Ripken, let me tell you about the four baseball jerseys I own and which I have hanging in my game room: Sandy Koufax, Nolan Ryan, Mickey Mantle, and Cal Ripken Jr. Ripken always played the game well and played it with gusto, durability, and class. In the outside world, he has handled himself the same way.

XXIII

DAVEY O'BRIEN

BALANCE

Happiness is not a matter of intensity,
but of balance and order and rhythm
and harmony.

—Thomas Merton

Replacing a legend—we've seen it time and again in sports.

Numerous examples come to mind: Phil Bengtson following Vince Lombardi at Green Bay; Gene Bartow replacing John Wooden at UCLA; Danny White taking the football from Roger Staubach for the Dallas Cowboys; Jim Nantz following Pat Summerall at CBS; Carl Yastrzemski moving into Ted Williams's spot in front of Boston's Green Monster; Bobby Murcer replacing Mickey Mantle; and Bobby Bonds (that's Barry's dad, for you youngsters) coming up behind Willie Mays.

Long before Lombardi was having trophies named after him or Ted Williams had retired to a life of leisure, another sports legend was replaced by an upstart intent on carving out a name for himself. The living legend was Texas Christian University quarterback Sammy Baugh, and his successor, Davey O'Brien, might have been small in stature (five feet seven, 150 pounds), but he was big at heart. He would go on to have a pretty good career himself, if winning a Heisman Trophy counts for something.

After leading the Horned Frogs to an undefeated season and the national title in 1938, his second year as a starter, O'Brien was named to thirteen All-American teams and became the first player to ever win the Heisman, Maxwell, and Walter Camp awards in the same season. When he went to New York City for the Heisman Trophy ceremony, he went to the Downtown Athletic Club in style, riding a stagecoach courtesy of a group of Fort Worth boosters. When's the last time you've heard of something like that?

Believe it or not, as long ago as O'Brien played, he was one of my dad's favorites. Why my dad, as a teenager up in Canada, even knew about the Texas native O'Brien who played his college days in Fort Worth still stymies me. It was probably because TCU won the national championship, and he came to admire O'Brien. Dad would later tell me that he admired O'Brien because he was such an overachiever. Davey O'Brien was the Doug Flutie of his day, an undersized player who overachieved (Flutie also won a Heisman Trophy). Not only that, O'Brien was a gentleman, and that's a word my father often used to describe someone who's polite, focused, committed, genuine, loyal, and hardworking. Put all those descriptive words together and you've got a very balanced individual. You've got Davey O'Brien. It's amazing how my dad could sense all that, as they didn't even have TV back then. But he had the goods on O'Brien.

In those days, when O'Brien was playing at TCU, there was no ESPN or even an ABC-TV game of the week in college football. In fact, there was no live television, period. Much was left to the imagination, where what you learned of college football was either seen at the local game or heard on the radio, as folks sat listening to a staticky broadcast of a game that had all the drama of whatever the play-by-play announcer could conjure up on his own.

It was easier to be a role model in those days because no one really knew you, except for what they heard and read about what you accomplished on the field. Still, I have to believe that O'Brien would have been a worthy role model to any generation, regardless of the media's prying.

Even after finishing out his playing days at TCU, O'Brien continued to chase Baugh. He signed with the Philadelphia Eagles out of college, and in his rookie year he passed for 1,324 yards in eleven games, breaking Baugh's National Football League record. He was named first-team quarterback for the NFL All-Star Team and got a $2,000 raise from the Eagles for 1940, only to retire after the following season to join the FBI. For good measure, in his last

NFL game, O'Brien completed thirty-three of sixty passes for 316 yards in a game against the Washington Redskins.

O'Brien spent ten years in the FBI, first as a firearms instructor at the bureau's field office in Springfield, Ohio, and then five years working out of Dallas. He retired from the FBI in 1950, to work in land development and then in the oil business. He was named to the College Football Hall of Fame in 1955 and the Texas Sports Hall of Fame in 1956.

Even though O'Brien was smaller than Baugh and probably not as gifted an athlete, he made up for it by being the consummate leader and ultimate teammate. Obviously, his smarts extended beyond the playing field, as evidenced by his joining the FBI. It certainly impressed my dad. He knew the importance of education, and I also remember reading the book *The FBI Story* upon the recommendation of my dad. No doubt Dad suggested it to me out of his admiration for O'Brien.

When I was a youngster, my parents always urged me to read. Not comic books or Web blogs but real books: biographies, sports stories, books on motivation and leadership. It's a rich experience that is timeless, turning the pages in your hands, anxious to get on with the book and discover what surprises and revelations are to be found "around the corner." Davey O'Brien was an educated man. My parents were always professing the importance of education. I learned at an early age that knowledge was the one thing that no one could ever take from you.

There was another personal connection of mine to O'Brien as well, in a roundabout way. I can remember as a young boy getting my hands on a TCU decal out of a cereal box promotion and keeping it because I liked the purple and white colors. There's no way I could have known at the time that not only would I someday be working in DFW but would also be covering the purple-and-white TCU Horned Frogs.

As you might have guessed, I never did get to meet O'Brien. He passed away from cancer in 1977, three years before I moved to Texas.

Shortly after O'Brien passed away, the Davey O'Brien Memorial Trophy was established, originally to be awarded to the Southwest Conference Player of the Year. The year after I moved to Texas, the award was changed to the national quarterback award (coming at the suggestion of noted college football announcer Keith Jackson, who felt the award's SWC ties made it too regional and lacking in the national impact that O'Brien himself had made some forty years earlier).

In hindsight, it was a great move; Keith "Oh, Nelly" Jackson was right on target. It's become one of the most prestigious awards in all of sports, not just college football. Jim McMahon, coming out of BYU, was the first recipient of the award following the change. In the last twenty-five years or so, "the Punky QB Known as McMahon" has come back for the annual awards ceremony all but twice, always wearing his trademark shades and sneakers, a wild tie, maybe some offbeat cufflinks (such as the "handcuff" ones his daughter once gave him for his birthday), and a tuxedo. Yes, always a tuxedo (at least from the waist up) and always sporting a smile.

Another BYU quarterback would soon win the O'Brien, and that was Steve Young. Like McMahon, Young is a terrific guy, fun to be around, and he's been so generous with his time. I got to know him not only through the O'Brien Award but also because of our mutual involvement with the Children's Miracle Network Telethon, which I hosted in North Texas in the 1980s and 1990s. After leading the 49ers to the Super Bowl title in 1994, Steve took the time to come on my *Sports Extra* program live with me from Miami, even though the game had ended much earlier. I was impressed, and grateful, that he would stick around to do the show with me when he could have been out celebrating with teammates, friends, and family. You don't forget things like that.

I had flown my parents in to be there for Super Bowl weekend, and they were as impressed with Young as I was. It's always been a hoot to hear my dad pontificate about one of his role models and all the great character attributes they possess—this even after I had been all grown up for many years (or at least I looked at it that way). Steve Young was now on my dad's list of good guys and positive role models, and that once you get on that list, it's pretty hard to fall off.

I began serving as master of ceremonies for the O'Brien Award ceremony in 1987 at the request of Charles Ringler, a longtime friend of Davey's who had founded the award named in honor of his good pal. Mr. Ringler (who has become a cherished friend) had been the emcee of the award ceremony since the award's inception, so I was pleased to be asked and humbly accepted when given the honor to assume his role.

The O'Brien Award has been very special for me, as well, because it has given me the chance to get to know some of the award winners. One such winner is Syracuse's Don McPherson, who won the O'Brien Award in 1987, while finishing runner-up to Tim Brown in the Heisman voting. This brings up an interesting point of trivia: Who are the only two Heisman winners that went to the same high school? Brown and O'Brien, who both went to Dallas' Woodrow Wilson High School.

McPherson is now the executive director of the Sports Leadership Institute at Adelphi University. I've gone with him to a couple of talks he's given at schools, and he's a terrific speaker. Extremely powerful, with a very meaningful message.

Another O'Brien winner I got to know quite well, which shouldn't be much of a surprise, is Troy Aikman, who won the award in 1988 and would end up carving out a nice NFL career in Dallas with the Cowboys—to include three Super Bowl titles.

The following year, Mr. Ringler asked me to become a member of the foundation's board of trustees, which was another event worthy of a phone call to Dad. He was not only excited on my behalf, but he took the occasion to retell many of the same Davey O'Brien stories he had shared with me when I was a kid. At the 1990 banquet, Mr. Ringler presented me with a treasure that

I certainly cherish: a beautiful bronze statue of Davey O'Brien, similar to the actual trophy itself, and it sits proudly in my study to this day.

I very much enjoy my continued involvement as master of ceremonies and board member of both the Davey O'Brien Foundation and SMU Athletic Forum board of trustees, which presents the Doak Walker Award winner each year. Both presentation banquets are done so well and so professionally. Being associated with two of the finest individuals ever to play football is a nice part of the whole package. And like the bronze O'Brien statue I was given, SMU President Dr. Gerald Turner not only presented me with a framed jersey with my name on it in recognition of my association with the Doak Walker Award and Southern Methodist University but also honored me with a bronze plaque that hangs in the school's football stadium.

Then there's Davey's son, David. He has remained involved with the foundation and in recent years has taken on a more active role as chairman of the high school scholarship award program. Just like his dad, David is quite a character and yet a perfect gentleman as well.

A couple of years ago, Archie Manning invited David and me to Oxford, Mississippi, to see his son Eli Manning in his last game at Ole Miss. The O'Brien Foundation had stayed close to the Mannings ever since older son Peyton had won the O'Brien in 1997 while at Tennessee. Peyton, like McMahon, has returned for many of the O'Brien Award ceremonies since winning, and he remains as committed, cordial, and courteous as any individual you'll ever meet. It was quite an experience to be with all the Mannings in Mississippi on a football Saturday.

There were close to one hundred thousand people there, with about 99 percent of them dressed to the nines, all assembled in a place they call "the Grove." I thought I had seen it all in going to college football games over the years, but this was special. Fine china. Fine food. Even the occasional candelabra hanging from the most elegant of temporary tents. Talk about classy. Another unforgettable sight was watching the Ole Miss seniors, about to play their final game, walk through the Grove to the applause and adulation of the families and fans who had gathered.

David and I were most impressed by all this, and while it was going on, I got to see another side of David—the very side Dad had told me about David's dad—how focused, committed, and balanced he was. David and his wife, Liz, are simply good people, and he lives the legacy of his dad, kind and caring.

David told me, "Dad never thought of himself as physically small, but, boy, was he ever competitive. Like the time he was beaten in a tavern in a game of darts. Later that day, on his way home, he stopped at a store and bought his own set of darts. He practiced for days until he was proficient and felt confident, then returned to the tavern and took on all comers. He never lost. But as competitive as he was, he put an incredibly high premium on friendship."

Having a famous father can have its drawbacks, often resulting in undue expectations and obligations. Yet David says that was never an issue when it came to his dad. "He never put any limitations on me. I can vividly remember going off to camp the summer of my sophomore year in high school. I wrote him a letter and told him I didn't want to pursue his love, football, but instead compete in track. A couple of days later, I got a letter back from him, assuring me that wasn't a problem, wishing me good luck. He always said just the right thing. I felt so good. After that, I always felt I could do whatever I wanted to do. We always had a great relationship. He was as loyal and modest a man as I have ever met."

Over the years, several of the O'Brien Award winners didn't even know who the award's namesake was until they won it, but their ears perk up when they learn that O'Brien won a Heisman.

One of the perks that comes from my involvement with the O'Brien Foundation and serving as chairman of the National Selection Award Committee is that I get to travel to Orlando, Florida, each December for the annual ESPN College Football Awards Show at Disney World, when the top collegiate football awards are announced on television as part of a two-hour live broadcast. It's always great to meet the new winners and to renew acquaintances with former winners and officials from the various award organizations. It's a fraternity of sorts, not to mention an opportunity to catch up with media cronies I've met over the years, all assembled in the land of make-believe.

Being involved with the foundation that bears the name Davey O'Brien is a reminder of a calmer, gentler time in our world, when our sports heroes truly were heroes. From the historic Fort Worth Club, where the awards presentation banquet is hosted each year, to the small-town feeling of the city of Fort Worth, to the memory of this man for whom this prestigious award is named, it's all a throwback to a time when things moved a little slower, people were a little kinder, and a man's word actually was his word. It's almost like a Norman Rockwell painting come to life. In fact, it's an awful lot like the stories Dad told me of what life was like when he was growing up.

Almost thirty years after his death and close to seventy years after he won the Heisman, Davey O'Brien endures because he was all those things dad told me about—polite, focused, committed, genuine, loyal, and hard-working. Truly a balanced individual. And then again, Dad could have just as well been talking about himself.

MAGIC JOHNSON

JOY

Sometimes your joy is the source of your smile, but sometimes your smile is the source of your joy.

—Thich Nhat Nanh

I am a basketball junkie. Always have been; always will be. Basketball was one of the first sports I got a chance to play on a regular basis as a little boy. It was so simple to play: All that's needed is a basketball (properly inflated, of course) and a basket or any kind of hoop that the ball can be shot through.

It's so simple, in fact, that I was able to start playing the sport with neither a basketball nor a backboard-mounted basket with a net. My first basketball "arena" consisted of a tennis ball and a makeshift hoop scotch-taped to the wall. That wasn't all. As crazy as it might sound, I even taped a makeshift basket on the back of the wastebasket in my bedroom so I could score every time I tossed a wadded-up piece of paper. Over the years, my aim got pretty darn deadly.

My bedroom was the site of many of my greatest moments in sports, where I could be anyone I wanted to be, able to achieve the improbable, sometimes the impossible.

How good was my shooting touch? Let me take you back in time, way back to when I was a freshman in high school, sitting near the back of the room in Mrs. Zuk's (yes, that was her real name) algebra class. As long ago as that was, and I won't even get into numbering the years, the seating arrangements weren't a whole lot different than I suppose they are now. We squeezed ourselves into cramped desks, with the deskfronts just about big enough to rest an open book with your elbows plated at either side, your arms capable of either writing out math problems, turning the pages, or resting your head when the teacher wasn't looking.

Every day I would go to Mrs. Zuk's class and sometimes would just sit there, staring ahead, daydreaming, glancing at that wastebasket next to her desk, about twenty feet away (just outside the college game's current three-point arc). The sentimental part of me remembers the chalk being applied to blackboards, the banging of the erasers, the alluring aroma of freshly mimeographed handouts or tests still wet with purple ink (the better so we could pick them up in our hands and sniff them), and shiny, wooden floors that were freshly lacquered every night. Then there was that silly trash can, calling my name, daring me to shoot away from "downtown."

Meanwhile, there was an ongoing battle raging inside of me, with my having to resist every urge I had to ball up a piece of paper and let fly from the back of the room. It was an inviting proposition, and, finally, one day I was no longer able to resist the temptation.

Just before the bell rang to signify the start of class, I grabbed a sheet of paper, wadded it up, and let loose with a long-range set shot, seated version. Nothing but net. Immediately, Mrs. Zuk yanked me, literally, out of my seat and shipped me off to the principal's office. It would be my only such trip in all my years of schooling, and it left me with a lingering case of guilt.

For me this was Basketball 101, the best class I ever took, much to the dismay of Mrs. Zuk.

When I got to his office, the principal, Mr. Tucker, was floored. He couldn't believe I, Mr. Straitlaced Student (I was Richie Cunningham before *Happy Days*), was even there. I told him what I had done, and all he said to me, fairly sternly, was to restrict my basketball shooting to the gym, where it belonged. "Why don't you stay here until the bell rings, then just go to your next class," he said. After I got home, down in the dumps, I spilled the whole story to my mom, and soon my dad was with us in the room. Mom was the disciplinarian in our household, so I had already been lightly scolded by her by the time Dad arrived home from his office. When he heard of my adventure, he calmly said, "Did you make it?" "I sure did, Dad."

"Well, make sure it's your last twenty-footer in the classroom. Do that out there," he said, pointing to the basketball hoop my parents had put up in our backyard.

Even though I was fairly short all through high school—I wouldn't reach my adult height of six feet until midway through college—I was a pretty decent basketball player. Quick and fast. Great from long range. I honed my game on that backyard hoop, which became a popular gathering spot for my friends and me, better for my parents to keep an eye on us during after-school hours.

Years earlier, as a youngster, I had played what they called Biddy Basketball. My best year in basketball came in that Biddy league, when I led the league in scoring and was named most valuable player. But what was lacking was the biggest prize of all, a league championship for my team. Worst, I didn't even get to play in the championship game. My grandfather—my dad's dad—passed away, and we had to go to Canada for the funeral, forcing me to miss the game. When I called and told my coach that my grandfather had died and I would have to miss the game, I couldn't tell if he felt worse about my family's loss or the loss of one of his starting players.

We lost the title game by four points in my absence. As for my grandfather, he had been the only grandfather I had known because my mother's dad had passed away many years earlier, when she was just nine years old. The grandfather I knew and loved meant a lot to me, so much so that I named my son, in part, after him. His first name is Doug, named after my dad, but his middle name is Eric, my grandfather's first name.

As decent a player as I was growing up, I saved my best games for my daydreams, on those countless days when I wore Celtic green and played alongside the likes of Tom Heinsohn, Bob Cousy, Bill Russell, K. C. Jones, Don Nelson, and Dave Cowens. And don't forget John Havlicek, "Hondo," "Perpetual Motion," the thirteen-time All-Star who gave 100 percent, 100 percent of the time.

Ironic, isn't it, that as much as I worshiped the Celtics, the basketball player I would come to admire the most was an avowed Celtics rival, Earvin "Magic" Johnson. Throughout the 1980s, Magic Johnson and Larry Bird comprised the biggest rivalry in sports, although it all started, really, in the 1979 NCAA title game, when Johnson's Michigan State team defeated Bird's previously undefeated Indiana State team, 75–64. It remains the highest-rated NCAA championship game in television ratings history, even though neither school had much of a championship legacy in basketball. The appeal was the incredible play and charisma exuded by both Johnson and Bird—especially the former, who was as comfortable with a microphone and a reporter's notebook in front of him as he was with a basketball in his hands.

There are a number of words that can be used to describe Johnson, and I pick "joy." I choose it because of the joy with which Johnson played the game, always hustling, able to play any position on the floor with such an élan (remember when he filled in for Kareem Abdul-Jabbar at center once in the play-offs, leading the Lakers to the NBA title?). His joy was the kind you associate with an artist who loves demonstrating his craft and gets as much a charge out of what he is able to pull off as does the spectator or patron who watches him do it. There also was great joy in watching Johnson, simply because he played with so much positive emotion, all the time, always like he was in a really great mood. And it rubbed off on those around him, taking them all to a higher level.

If all of us could emulate Johnson-like joy in our work, in our professions, I dare say the world would be a better place. Certainly starting with our own world.

I was the television play-by-play man for the Dallas Mavericks in the team's second season, which was the year the Mavs took three players (Mark Aguirre, Rolando Blackman, and Jay Vincent) in the first twenty-four selections. Vincent was a small forward out of Michigan State and had been a teammate of Johnson's at MSU, so through Jay I was able to glean a lot of tidbits about Magic—stuff I could use in my broadcasts whenever the Mavs played the Lakers.

But it wasn't like he was a stranger to me. I had spoken a lot with Johnson during pregame interviews as well as in the locker room after games, so I was quite familiar with how personable and accommodating he was. I would even get to "coach" him at times, as one of the celebrity coaches in Spud Webb's Annual All-Star Game, benefiting a local chapter of the Boys and Girls Club in Dallas. We would hold a draft of the players, and, as luck would have it, I usually got the first pick and would always select Magic.

As much as Johnson could turn on a crowd and do amazing things on the basketball court, there was nothing phony or pretentious about him.

He was sincere to every fan who wanted his attention. Teammates liked him and respected him (as well they should, considering that Johnson had a lot to do with the Lakers winning five NBA titles while he played for them). He simply had fun with the game, showing his joy for the sport, which in the days of Magic and Bird and, later, Michael Jordan, was a better-played game—truly a team game—than the version we are now subjected to, the eyesore that rewards individuality and suffocates the artistry.

When it comes to admiring Magic Johnson, don't take my word for it. Here's what my son Doug says about the greatest six-foot-nine guard ever to play the game:

"At a Spud Webb Celebrity Charity Game, it was either 1988 or '89, when I was a ball boy, I asked Magic to sign a picture of the Lakers logo on a yellow sheet of cardboard (which I still have framed to this day). This was before the game itself and right before the guys went out to the court. He had just finished an interview and was hurrying out, when I showed him the picture and asked him to sign it. He was in a hurry to get out onto the court and really didn't have any time to stop, but he promised me that after the game he would find me in the locker room and sign my picture. I got the sense that he might have been impressed by the fact that I had taken the time to draw the logo. I was just happy that he had said anything.

"After the game I was in the locker room getting some autographs from the players and other celebrities, when I heard someone asking me where the picture was, and I turned around and saw Magic standing there. He asked if he could sign the picture I had shown him earlier. He even asked if it was okay to sign over the logo or if I wanted him to write around it, as he wanted to make sure he wouldn't mess up my drawing. It was just one of the most amazing experiences of my life because Magic Johnson, who was already my favorite basketball player, had remembered me and made such an effort to keep a promise to a little ballboy.

"I also remember sitting in my dorm room at Baylor University only two or three years after that All-Star Game, watching TV, when there was a break-in for a special report. Magic was at the podium, and he said that he was having to retire from basketball immediately. It was such a big shock, and I remember calling my best friend from high school, whose hero was Magic, and breaking the news to him. It was such a surreal event, watching one of my heroes leaving the game way too early. All I could do was think back to that night he had signed the picture for me.

"Most athletes have no idea the effect they can have on someone, young or old. They can leave an everlasting impression, good or bad, without even being aware of it."

I remember Johnson's announcement that he had tested positive for HIV like it was yesterday, even though it has been fifteen years since. I was in the middle of taping a *Scott's Kids* segment at Will Rogers Coliseum, when I got a call on my new cell phone (that I had forgotten to turn off while taping). I was upset that I would have to start the taping over again, until I answered the phone and quickly forgot about any inconvenience. It was the TV station calling me, telling me I had to come in as soon as possible, that Magic had announced his retirement and his health situation, and we would need to chase the story.

I tried to collect my thoughts in the fifteen-minute drive back to the station. Much of America took it as though it were bad news in their own families, and on top of that there was the realization that when someone admitted he or she was HIV positive, death was right around the corner. Think Rock Hudson.

Magic had been admired for so long—better than a decade—as someone so talented and yet so committed to being a positive influence in people's lives. Now there was this, and it was easy to then start passing judgment on Johnson, even though all of us have skeletons in the closet we never want let out. Johnson could no longer hide the fact he had cheated on his wife and now had a potentially deadly disease that carried a terrible stigma.

I was on the air plenty that day, among other things answering questions from anchors who were aware of the fact that I had come to know Johnson quite well. What was the real story? How devastating would this be to his family? Would he be okay? They all wanted to know.

Fifteen years later, I continue to be amazed that Magic is as healthy as he is. I've served as the master of ceremonies at a number of events that have raised money and awareness for HIV/AIDS, and each time I couldn't help but think of the impact Magic Johnson has brought to the disease. In that sense, he's done for HIV/AIDS awareness what Mickey Mantle did for organ transplants. Both men, for a time the best at their respective games, paid for the sins of their past and yet had the fortitude to turn their respective predicaments into public service.

Johnson took that scary moment in November 1991 and turned it into his defining moment. He committed himself to making it right. His Magic Johnson Foundation continues to thrive to this day with assistance for health issues, educational concerns, and social needs of inner-city youth. As I write this, Abbott Laboratories, which deals with many of the drugs used to assist those with HIV/AIDS, has signed on Johnson as a spokesperson as part of its HIV/AIDS research program. His foundation will team with Abbott to create educational platforms in cities with a huge prevalence of HIV infection.

Aside from his foundation, Magic has become quite the businessman and entrepreneur, under the umbrella of Magic Johnson Enterprises. Through the years, I have attended a number of openings for his new ventures, ranging from Starbucks, to Burger King, to Magic Johnson 24-Hour Fitness Clubs, to Magic Johnson Theatres. Each time, that contagious, unmistakable grin of joy is there to greet you.

So, what is it that has allowed Magic to be so magic? Quite simply, his personality. He's inspirational, motivational, and magical all rolled up into one. That's why corporate America continues to be fascinated with him. He walks into a room, and immediately it lights up. Few have his charisma, his appeal, his infectious smile, and his pleasing personality.

Nobody knows better what Magic brought to a team than Jerry West, the Lakers general manager during their four NBA titles in the decade of the '80s. "He absolutely loved the game and brought a very special joy to it."

Despite his six-foot-nine frame, he never gives you the impression he is towering over you. There are few people I've ever known who have such magnetism. You are simply drawn to him, just like his teammates at the high school, college, and pro levels were drawn to him. He simply loves life and the joy it can bring. One of his favorite sayings, derived from the words of the late president John F. Kennedy, speaks volumes about the joy he gets from helping others take their abilities to the next level. "Ask not what your teammates can do for you; ask what you can do for your teammates." That's Magic Johnson.

So many high-profile athletes want to make a difference and should be making a difference, but they don't always succeed—at least not like Magic. Just as my mother would always say, there is a reason for everything. You can't help but wonder if Magic was put on this earth not only to entertain us with all his great basketball talents, but maybe, even more importantly, to be a spokesman and carry a torch for those in underprivileged environments, dysfunctional families, or medically challenged worlds. It's obvious he truly enjoys helping those in need.

As amazed as I am with his athletic triumphs and his admission of real-life shortcomings, what has impressed me the most has been his willingness to take on any and all challenges thrown at him. Call it service with a smile. A Magic smile of joy.

BART CONNER

&

NADIA COMANECI

PERFECTION

Perfection has to do with the end product, but excellence has to do with the process.

—Jerry Moran

M ention the name Nadia Comaneci to me, and my thoughts drift back to Montreal, Quebec, site of the 1976 Summer Olympics. Those were the first Olympic Games I ever got to see in person. What was truly unforgettable about them was getting to see Comaneci, then a fourteen-year-old sensation from Romania, score the first perfect 10 in Olympic gymnastics competition.

She didn't get just one 10 either; she scored seven of them—four times on the bars and three times on the beam. Her heavy-medal haul in Montreal consisted of three gold medals, one silver, and one bronze. Before Nadia, no gymnast had even achieved the ultimate score of 10.0. In fact, the scoreboard in Montreal was not designed to accommodate perfection. Instead, a 1.00 had to be displayed whenever she scored a 10.

Eight years before Mary Lou Retton was scoring ten at Los Angeles in 1984, Comaneci was staking her claim to the original Ms. Ten, a level of perfection that should be a worthy goal for all of us to achieve in whatever we do. But life really isn't about being perfect, about setting standards so high that we put relentless pressure on ourselves and set ourselves up for perpetual disappointment. But the "perfection" spoken of here is meant only as an ideal to strive for while being the best that you can be. Thank goodness my parents never expected me to be perfect, and they never tried to lay that on me as some sort of hardcore motivational ploy.

Four turbulent years after Montreal, this time in Moscow—following a period of her life which included her parents divorcing, her noticeable weight gain, the removal of the renowned Bela Karolyi as her coach, her skipping the 1978 Romanian Nationals, her linking back up with Karolyi, and a variety of medical problems—Comaneci rebounded to win a gold in both beam and floor, and a silver in vault.

Over two Olympiads, Comaneci won a total of five golds, three silvers, and one bronze. Every Olympics, it seems, has its designated darling competitor, and for one at least (the 1976 Montreal Games), Comaneci was that golden girl: too young to date and too limber and powerful to believe for someone a few bricks shy of a hundred pounds.

When I went to those Montreal Games, I was a young buck in my twenties, still in the early days of carving out a career in broadcast journalism. I was learning what television news was all about. In those days it was all about making the transition from film to videotape. It's almost laughable now to even talk about things such as film and videotape when both kinds of technology by today's standards are the equivalent of sticks and stones.

While I had grown up outside Rochester, New York, a short day's drive from Montreal, I had never been to that wonderful city until going to those Olympic Games in 1976. Even before I went, the city had great sentimental value for me, as my parents had honeymooned there.

Comaneci was incredible. So disciplined, so respectful, so good. Nobody could touch her. She was perfection at its finest. And to think that she had never appeared in an Olympic Games before. Give a lot of the credit to Karolyi as well, the burly, thickly mustachioed coach who would himself become a household name.

Nadia would continue to compete in gymnastics for a little while beyond the 1980 Games, and she would save some of her best for the last. At the 1981 World University Games, held in her native country of Romania, Comaneci won all five gold medals, and she would officially retire from the sport several years later, in 1984, at age twenty-two. She was awarded the prestigious Olympic Order by Juan Antonio Samaranch, the president of the International Olympic Committee,

By then, though, she was no longer the darling of the gymnastic world who could practically slither her way through keyholes if she had to. She was starting to blossom and fill out as a beautiful woman, a phenomenon no less striking today as she turns forty-five in 2006.

Except for a brief, strictly monitored appearance by Comaneci at L.A.'s 1984 Olympic Games, the Western public rarely saw Nadia. Because of her global popularity, especially in America, Romania's communist leadership considered her a prime candidature for defection. Forbidden to travel, she settled into her new career as a gymnastics coach, although in November 1989 she would finally flee Romania and eventually make her way to the United States, where she settled.

Before getting to America, though, Nadia spent the first year or two of her newfound freedom in Canada, living with former Romanian rugby coach Alexandru Stefu and his wife, and it was there that Comaneci would work herself back into shape for some gymnastics exhibitions, which gave her the chance to reacquaint herself with Bart Conner. Conner eventually became a close phone pal of Nadia's and invited her to move to Norman, Oklahoma, where he owned a gymnastics academy. In 1994 he proposed marriage and she accepted, and in April 1996 they were married in a civil ceremony in Romania, followed by a church wedding the next day.

Bart himself was a great gymnast. Despite having to come back from a second torn-biceps injury, he won two gold medals at the 1984 Games, and from there he would forge a career as a terrific TV commentator for gymnastics coverage. Bart is as smooth an analyst as he is photogenic, and he's a natural when it comes to TV. In fact, he's a perfect 10 as well! Bart, just like Nadia had, scored a pair of 10s at the 1984 Games in the parallel bars.

Bart loves to be the jokester, always a smile on his face to go with that pleasant disposition, and never too shy to inform you of the great success that he and Nadia have enjoyed in gymnastics, winning a total of eleven Olympic medals. Then, with a deadpan face, Bart adds, "Nadia won nine; I won two."

Bart and Nadia really are an extraordinary couple. Today they work together in running the gymnastics academy that Bart helped start, and both do a lot of motivational speaking, among other endeavors. On a couple of occasions they have helped me out by coming down from Oklahoma to serve as honorary hosts for charity events.

Many of those commitments will, at least for the foreseeable future, now be put on hold. That's because Bart and Nadia have become parents of their own "perfect 10" with the birth of their first child, Dylan Paul, on June 3, 2006. "He already has definition in his deltoids and his biceps," announced a proud dad. "We've been through a lot of high moments in our life in sports through what we accomplished but this is just something that is totally unique," added an equally proud mom.

One thing Bart and I have in common—and I can assure you that it's not gymnastic ability—is that we both like fast cars. Not the kind of fast driving that piles up speeding tickets, mind you, but the sporting kind that involves a racetrack. In fact, Bart was always a celebrity driver at my annual charity legends event held at Texas Motor Speedway. He's also done some television segments with me and has appeared on my radio show. We all have a common bond with the Muscular Dystrophy Association. I cohosted the annual Jerry Lewis Labor Day MDA Telethon in DFW for twenty-five years and served as a member of the MDA board of directors. Bart has done the same in Chicago for years, and both he and Nadia remain members of the national board of trustees. Therefore, it's always great renewing our friendship at national MDA Telethon host meetings each year.

As you might have guessed, I really feel blessed to have become close friends with both Bart and Nadia. They are so real. No hidden agendas, no haughty attitudes, simply genuine folks. Nadia is such a bubbly personality who really has joy in her life and doesn't mind letting people know about it. She is so different from that stoic, almost-grim-faced little girl we remember from the 1976 Olympic Games. Years later, despite her Romanian accent, Nadia is as American as any other girl next door. In fact, she became a naturalized citizen of the United States several years ago. Every time I see her and Bart, they are always looking to have fun and make a difference. Always smiles. Always hugs. Always good people. For sure, two perfect 10s.

XXVI

LANCE ARMSTRONG

ENDURANCE

Endurance is one of the most difficult disciplines, but it is to the one who endures that the final victory comes.

—Buddha

There is so much about Lance Armstrong that hits home with me. It would be possible to talk about him for hours without touching on any of the details of his seven Tour de France victories. I couldn't begin to tell you what his biggest margin of victory was, how many stages he actually won, or how many total miles he has ridden while wearing the yellow jersey.

I can't tell you what make of bike he used, the exact tactics he employed in the hills and mountains that enabled him to pass so many other racers, or where his training regimen ranks in terms of the sport's all-time-greatest bike racers.

Yet, this much I do know: Armstrong might have been the best there ever was at a sport, and in its premier event, that rewards endurance more than any other quality. The Tour de France is a daily, three-week event that covers more than two thousand miles, much of it up (and then down) steep, twisting mountain roads as perilous as they are wondrous. It's being winded to the nth degree, your thighs screaming from lactic acid, your arms aching through to every fiber, your mind boggled by the relentless strategy of dealing with dozens of other bikers around you, all in the same kind of pristine, tip-top condition that you are in.

Imagine doing this for five, six, sometimes seven hours a day, much of that time spent hunkered down over your handlebars, your rear rammed against a seat far removed from the comfort of that sleep-inducing sofa you cozy up on back home. Bike racers sometimes do all this in a rainy drizzle, knowing every second that one little bump from another rider or slipped tire on slickened pavement could send you careening down a steep embankment on either side of the hairpin turn you are trying to negotiate.

Endurance? How about spending the better part of two years fighting for your life against a virulent form of cancer that has spread from your testicles to your brain, every moment of your life clinging to the tiniest of hopes that you will survive to race another day. Tour de France? How about Tour de Cancer?

Any heartfelt conversation about Armstrong begins with the fact that he is a cancer survivor. He was only in his twenties when, in October 1996, he was told by a doctor that he had testicular cancer. His odds of survival were put at less than 40 percent. Here's a confident, some say cocky, young guy who as a teenager had competed on equal footing against some of the world's best triathletes and cyclists but was now facing a possible death sentence.

"I'll never forget the doctor walking into the examining room and saying I had cancer," Armstrong told me. "I said, 'Are you sure?' And he said, 'I'm so sure that you're scheduled for surgery at seven in the morning.' I said, 'I guess you're sure.'

"It was such a surprise, even after he said the word 'cancer.' You don't expect it. You don't want it. You go into denial and depression. But I also knew I had a choice—give in or fight like hell. And that's what I did. I fought like hell. I drove home and immediately began thinking that even though I had only a 40 percent chance of survival, that was better than 10 percent or zero percent. And I held on to that nugget of hope. That became my race. The illness was my competition.

"I was the good guy; cancer was the bad guy. I fought constantly."

Up until Armstrong was diagnosed with cancer, he was known pretty much as a terrific athlete who hadn't quite hit the big time yet. As a teenager growing up in Plano, Texas, raised by a single mom, Linda, who would become his best friend, Armstrong wasn't your typical Texas jock. He wasn't a stud football player, didn't play basketball, and was not the type of guy cut out to be on the golf course following in the footsteps of fellow Texans such as Byron Nelson and Ben Hogan.

At age thirteen he won the Rainbo Ironkids Triathlon, an accomplishment which first brought him to my attention. The folks at Rainbo were aggressive marketers, and they did a great job in managing to get video clips and a press packet into my hands so I'd promote the local kid on my nightly TV sportscast. Within three or four years of that, he was competing in world-class triathlons against the renowned likes of Scott Tinley and Mark Allen. When he finished among the top three or four men at an elite triathlon at Las Colinas outside Dallas, Armstrong, short but solid in his Speedo and wraparound sunglasses, looked like a mini-Terminator, his chest puffed out as he spoke to reporters at the finish line, his persona bold and matter of fact, proof that he belonged on a world-sports stage.

Still, when 1996 rolled around, by which time Armstrong had long since decided to focus on cycling, he wasn't a household name. He had been a member of the U.S. Olympic cycling team at the 1996 Games in Atlanta, but other than that, at best, he was a second-tier athlete. He was a bit of a maverick by then, living in Austin and known around town, in his own words, as something of a slacker not driven to get the best out of his incredible athletic talent.

One of the things about individual sports—cycling, swimming, track, and figure skating—that differs from team sports is that it's you against the world. Even if you have an entourage or a great support group, no one but you is responsible for how you perform once you are out on stage. When it comes to crunch time, there are no excuses. There's no finger pointing.

When I think of individual-sport athletes, I am always reminded of the Olympics. Incredible performers like Michael Johnson, Dominique Moceanu, Carl Lewis, and Lance Armstrong. Nineteen ninety-six in Atlanta was the first Olympics I would get a chance to report on Lance. But that summer, it was the bombing at Centennial Park that took center stage. So, instead of simply covering all-world performances, I ended up pulling all-nighters covering breaking stories as well.

Yet, I can only imagine that Lance had a lot more sleepless nights than I ever did after he got his cancer prognosis. I had an idea of what he was about to go through. My own younger sister, Debby, was in her thirties when she learned she had cancer. Within eleven months she was gone, leaving behind a husband, a son, a mother, a father, a sister, and a brother. It's never easy. Although you might learn to cope with it, you never totally accept it, and you never really get over it. It changed my parents for the rest of their lives: my mom's best friend was no longer there; my dad's little girl was gone.

It isn't meant to happen that way, but cancer has a way of changing things. Just ask Lance Armstrong. I was able to share stories with Lance's mom, Linda, and it was obvious that she felt incredibly blessed that she had been spared and that Lance had survived. By the time Lance was diagnosed, he was ranked No. 1 in the world, but the cancer had spread to his lungs and brain. He was forced to take a hiatus from racing as he underwent a couple of risky operations to remove cancerous tissue from his brain. He then had to withstand an aggressive chemotherapy treatment. While all this was going on, he started up the Lance Armstrong Foundation to help cancer sufferers. Even when he was too sick some days to get out of bed, Armstrong had the wherewithal to summon the energy and act on the desire to form his foundation. This was a precursor to how tough he would be when it came to getting back on his bike.

Boy, did he survive, going on to become perhaps one of the greatest athletes the world will ever know. Not only is Armstrong a survivor, to this day he remains an inspiration to millions who deal not only with cancer but adversity at any level. When Lance won his first Tour de France in 1999, his was a mission that had been transformed into a miracle.

A few years later in a one-on-one interview I did with Lance in front of fifteen hundred people at "The Conversation with a Living Legend" luncheon, benefiting the MD Anderson Cancer Center in Houston, he said a lot of profound things straight from the gut. He said that cancer had been the best thing that had ever happened to him, that it had been a wake-up call. He admitted he had not been as motivated as he should have been in the early '90s, when he was giving only 80–90 percent.

He said, "I had money, a brand-new Porsche, and a great house, but in Austin I was known as a slacker. I didn't focus on my job. I didn't give it 100 percent. That isn't right. It's wrong. I thought to myself, 'If I get another chance and beat this cancer, I'm always going to give it my all.' Cancer gave me an incredible perspective on life. I would never have won numerous Tour de France titles, let alone one, had I not gotten cancer."

Lance believed that in his battle with cancer, knowledge was power and attitude was everything. That mindset, coupled with some of the best medical knowledge, equipment, and physicians available at MD Anderson, allowed him to beat the disease. It took tremendous willpower for Armstrong to persevere through the agony and his debilitating condition, so that when he came out healthy on the other end, he was equipped to be an even better racer than he had been before. The steep mountain climbs were practically nothing compared to what he had been through. He had reached a whole new level of endurance.

Cancer had given Lance an edge he had never had before. He has never been a religious person, and when I asked him about whether or not his inner strength had come from a belief in a higher power, he said what had worked best for him was putting his faith in the hands of the doctors and the medical science available to him.

He said that every time a doctor told him that he was improving, it was like looking at a ballpark scoreboard and seeing himself ahead, 40–0. More good news would make it 50–0. "I constantly played those kinds of games to keep myself focused and challenged," he said.

In 2004, the Lance Armstrong Foundation unveiled its LIVESTRONG™ program, and soon yellow wristbands engraved with "LIVESTRONG" were popping up all over America. They were a testament to the message that

Lance was sharing, and still shares, about courage and survival in the face of death. More than $50 million has been raised by the foundation, which shows a lot of participation, considering that the wristbands cost only a dollar apiece.

After winning the 2005 Tour de France for his seventh consecutive victory in bicycling's most prestigious race, Armstrong retired from racing. But he'll never retire his efforts to promote and bring about awareness of cancer. He's not a cancer statistic; he's a cancer survivor, and he's proud of it.

"You can't live your life as a famous athlete forever," Armstrong told me. "We all see athletes become addicted to the game, the fame, the privileges they receive, and that's a mistake. Sports will come and go, but this is an illness that isn't just coming and going. It's here. I'll live with that forever.

"If I could bottle up the perspective I got from having cancer and just give it away, it would be an incredible gift to the world. To have that view on life, on difficulty, on crisis—crisis is an opportunity. Believe me, cancer was the best thing that ever happened to me. I was lucky to have that little bottle. Every single day, we have to look at our life like it's a gift."

Hearing that is my wake-up call. Let it be yours, too.

XXVII

DALLAS COWBOYS

1992–93

TEAMWORK

Coming together is a beginning . . . keeping together is progress . . . working together is success.

—Henry Ford

My dad has long been a huge advocate of the concept of "TEAM," the one in which individuals are subservient to the greater good. "Together, Everybody Achieves More," Dad would often say. He was forever reminding me to do my part; yes, be the best that I can be, but never forget that all the individual success in the world means nothing if the team doesn't win.

"Take care of your own role, and as long as everyone else does the same, things will fall into place," my father further explained.

Things sure fell into place for the Dallas Cowboys teams of 1992 and 1993, and some of my most enjoyable moments as a sportscaster include covering those teams. It sounds so obvious to be saying that, in light of the fact that both of those Jimmy Johnson–coached teams won Super Bowls. Easy to say, but there was nothing easy about how those Cowboys got to that point.

Great teams are those whose whole is greater than the sum of their parts. Teamwork involves intangibles, such as mutual trust and open communications, that can take a gathering of good talent—even mediocre in some spots—and produce great results measured in wins and losses, division titles, and league and world championships. Another word that comes to mind is *chemistry,* present on teams whose individuals enjoy the bus ride together back to the hotel instead of taking separate taxis. Teamwork is subservience of self and selfish ambition to the greater good of coming together to defeat an opponent, much more often than not.

There have been more overall-talented Dallas Cowboys teams than the ones that won three Super Bowls in the first half of the 1990s. Arguably, some of the Cowboys teams of the early 1980s might have had a higher level of talent if you added up the four-star ratings of each of their players, but none of those teams did so much as make it to a Super Bowl game, let alone win one.

There are classic cases of teams in other sports as well that represent self-sacrifice for the good of the team, and others that stand as examples of the opposite. The 2004 Boston Red Sox, for example, who reversed "the Bambino Curse" and brought Beantown its first World Series title in eighty-six years are among the former. The team, a band of self-proclaimed "idiots," bonded, pulled for one another, and did the little sacrificial things all season long that made a difference in a game here and a game there, and those add up.

That same season and through 2005, this was getting to be an old story. Right alongside the Red Sox in the same American League were the vaunted New York Yankees, presumably the greatest gathering of superstar talent that George Steinbrenner's money could buy. That Yankees team had a roster payroll of more than $200 million—over $50 million more than the next highest-paid team—but the best those Bronx Bombers could do was manage a runner-up finish to the Red Sox in the AL Championship Series. Those Yankees had great individual stats from the likes of Alex Rodriguez, Derek Jeter, and Jason Giambi, but as a group they were lacking in areas such as heart and servant-leadership. As of this writing, it had been since 2001 that a Yankees team had won a World Series title, even though year after year they have undoubtedly fielded the deepest team of individual stars in the entire major leagues.

Then there are those Cowboys teams of the Jimmy Johnson years. Consider this: in the first post-Landry season in 1989, the Cowboys went 1–15, often flailing around behind rookie quarterback Troy Aikman. His most memorable moment that season was being on the bench while fellow rookie quarterback Steve Walsh started in what would be the Cowboys' only victory of the season: over the Redskins, in Washington, D.C.

In three short seasons, though, the Cowboys went from worst to first. They did it with a couple of smart trades, some good drafts, and the occasional free-agent signing, with the newfangled braintrust of, chiefly, owner Jerry Jones and Coach Johnson piecing together a team that would remain intact, for the most part, long enough to put together a mini-dynasty. Jones's Cowboys would end up winning three Super Bowls over a four-year stretch, the third with Barry Switzer as coach.

Don't get the wrong idea, though. Johnson was the chief architect of all this, although Jones, as self-appointed general manager, played his proactive part in making all this happen.

The first piece of the puzzle had been put in place by the previous regime, when the Cowboys used their first-round pick on wide receiver Michael Irvin, at the time, ironically, one of Johnson's chief playmakers with the University of Miami Hurricanes. Irvin was a big presence who played bigger than six-foot-two, 210-pound frame, and had a great knack for not only getting open, but for fighting off defensive backs to make the tough grabs in traffic.

Irvin knew what it took to be a champion. He had learned at the University of Miami, where he was part of the 1987 Hurricanes team that won the national title under Johnson. By the time Irvin was done playing at Miami, he had set school records for receptions, receiving yards, and touchdown receptions. Already flashy and known for his rebellious streak, Irvin was picked eleventh overall by the Cowboys in the 1988 NFL draft.

Irvin was every bit as flamboyant in person by the time he got to Dallas as he was by reputation. He had been All-American in some eyes, All-Mouth in others. As likeable as he was, and certainly comfortable in front of the media, Michael proved to be a liability at times to the team. He was his own worst enemy, and it was easy to learn from watching Irvin, that when you don't make good decisions, you won't get good results. With all his rough edges, the best thing Irvin had going for him was getting to play for Johnson for five seasons. Johnson understood Irvin, and as long as it was him keeping tabs on his star receiver, Irvin would be fine.

That was the thing about Johnson, who, like me, had majored in psychology; he was a master at reading his players and knowing which buttons to push. Jimmy was the great motivator (and great manipulator when necessary), a master at playing with players' minds in just the right way to get them to perform better. It was fascinating watching Johnson work.

Irvin would go on to have a Pro Football Hall of Fame–caliber career with the Cowboys (although his off-field problems have kept him from getting elected as of this writing). Perhaps his best season came after Johnson left and was replaced by Barry Switzer. In 1995, Irvin set an NFL record with eleven consecutive games of one hundred or more yards receiving, finishing the season with career bests of 111 receptions and 1,603 receiving yards as the Cowboys went on to win another Super Bowl.

Aikman was the classic example of someone who benefited from playing for Johnson, although he couldn't have known at the time, considering what he went through his rookie season in Dallas in 1989. The Cowboys drafted Aikman out of UCLA with the No. 1 pick overall, thus giving Irvin, at least, a prototypical strapping quarterback with a strong arm, able to read defenses and pick apart secondaries. But despite all of Aikman's obvious talents and assets, Johnson wasn't going to make it easy on him. Not much later, Johnson got his hands on his star quarterback at Miami, Steve Walsh, thanks to a supplemental draft that gave the Cowboys an instant quarterback controversy.

I'll never forget that. I remember calling my dad and his saying, "Now that's a test for Aikman. Now you'll get a chance to see how strong Aikman is. If he's up to the task and takes the challenge, he'll survive. If he doesn't, No. 1 pick or not, Jimmy will go with his guy (Walsh), his quarterback from Miami he knows and trusts—Jimmy already knows that Steve will put it on the line for him."

Troy not only had to prove it to himself that he could survive the challenge, but he had to prove it to his coach as well, and it seemed obvious Johnson wasn't bluffing by bringing in Walsh. The early going wasn't easy for Troy, but like my dad had said, "Complaining about it doesn't cut it; performing does." That kind of attitude paid off for Aikman. Although it was Walsh who played quarterback in the Cowboys' only victory of 1989, Aikman kept persevering and improving, eventually ending up where he had started off when first drafted—as the Dallas quarterback of the future. Walsh would soon be gone, traded the next season to the New Orleans Saints. Once again, my dad had been right on the money.

Acquiring both Aikman and Walsh had been a no-lose proposition for Johnson. If Walsh was able to push Aikman into becoming an even better, more assured player, then Johnson would eventually get the star quarterback he needed to lift the Cowboys out of their rabbit hole. On the other hand, had Aikman buckled under the heat, Johnson knew that, in Walsh, he had a good Plan B, a quarterback accustomed to him, and vice versa, and one who knew what it felt like to win a lot of big games. Walsh was not a classic strong-armed quarterback, although he had the wiles to succeed in the NFL with the right coach and supporting cast.

To this day, I sometimes find myself wondering what would have happened in an alternate universe, had Aikman not worked out and Johnson been forced to go with Walsh for at least a few years.

Aikman recently told me that 1989 was the toughest year of his life. "Not winning is no fun," he said, adding, however, that he learned a lot from the experience, and it probably served to make him stronger later in his career, as he was then prepared for just about anything. In effect, Johnson had toughened up his young quarterback prodigy, doing it all with a masterful plan of psychology.

Unlike his favorite receiver Irvin, Aikman would make it to the Pro Football Hall of Fame in his first year of eligibility, getting elected in 2006 to a cherished spot in Canton, Ohio. There was no denying Aikman's worthiness of a Canton bust. He passed for more than thirty-two thousand yards in a twelve-year career that includes six Pro Bowls, a Super Bowl MVP, and those three Super Bowl championships.

Aikman was only thirty-four when he retired after the 2000 season, meaning he probably could have gone over forty thousand passing yards by playing just three or four more seasons. But as was the case with one of his predecessors and future business partners, Roger Staubach, Aikman had suffered numerous concussions, and for the good of his long-term health, he got out of football.

If there's anything to be learned from Troy Aikman, and there is plenty, it's that a combination of passion and perseverance goes a long way. He said his dad would often tell him, "If you work hard and stick to it, there is nothing in life you can't achieve." Obviously, Troy's dad and my dad had come out of the same school of thought.

Troy said he had wanted to be a pro athlete from the time he was eight years old. Okay, so that alone didn't make him that much different from other kids that age, but how he acted on that dream made him unique. He went to work and not just play. To make that dream a reality, Aikman knew what it would take. He told me that after Friday night high school basketball games, he wouldn't go out with his buddies. Instead, he would ask the coach for the keys to the weight room and go lift weights until one thirty Saturday morning. "I knew at an early age what it would take if I wanted to play professionally."

Aikman's dedication is evident in more than just the game he played. This is a guy who "gets it." Throughout the years, Troy has endeared himself to the community by giving back, over and over again. I was on the board of trustees of the Cook Children's Hospital when he launched his "Aikman's Endzone" concept. It involved an interactive playroom for kids, with plenty of toys, sports stuff, and computers that would link them through the Internet with hospitalized boys and girls in other cities. It was an incredible venture done in conjunction with movie director Steven Spielberg's Starbright Foundation. "Aikman's Endzones" are now in children's hospitals in Dallas, Fort Worth, and Oklahoma City, as Troy and his lovely wife, Rhonda, remain generous and involved with a number of worthy nonprofits.

As a ballplayer, Troy understood the whole media thing. He usually made himself easily accessible for interviews, live shots, television specials—stuff like that. His answers to reporters' questions were always informative and insightful. Still, it was his continued commitment, work ethic, and perseverance that would set him apart from many of his peers. At the same time, just like one of his predecessors, Roger Staubach, Aikman started dabbling in the corporate world while still playing, so that when he was ready to retire from football, the transition to the real world would be smooth.

That preparation has served him well, as he now has a successful car dealership and has emerged as one of the top football analysts on network television, these days teaming with FOX's lead announcer, Joe Buck. Then there's his venture with Staubach as co-owner of the Hall of Fame NASCAR Nextel Cup racing team, sponsored by Texas Instruments. Troy is smart and has already proven to be a shrewd businessman. He knows how the system works, and he's put it to good use for himself and those around him.

And the relationship between the two Hall of Fame quarterbacks doesn't stop there. They have teamed up for over a decade, scoring millions in dollars for the Children's Cancer Fund, serving as the honorary hosts at the annual Celebrity Style Show and Luncheon. Tell me that seeing Troy and Roger, each escorted by a child that is battling for his or her young life, doesn't open up hearts and checkbooks. How many athletes can you think of who have been able to take the incredible success they enjoyed on the field of play and then been able to transcend that great success into the real world, without ever missing a beat. Say hello to Aikman and Staubach.

Troy says it wasn't a loss of talent that caused the Cowboys to start sliding backward after winning their third Super Bowl in four years. It was a lack of commitment on the part of a select few who remained. They weren't focused on what should have been their number one priority, which was to play football and compete at the highest level possible. Like my dad had long said, if each individual does his job to the best of his ability, it's amazing the heights that can be attained collectively. It's everyone, together, rising to another level. That's what sets the victors apart.

The next player Dallas selected in the draft behind Aikman in 1989 was Syracuse's Daryl Johnston, the consummate over-achieving fullback. Likewise, he was always prepared, most dedicated, and passionate. In his playing days, even when he was hurt, you'd never know about it. He never whined or complained; he simply got the job done and was gracious doing it. Go ask Emmitt Smith who helped him get hundreds of additional yards over the years because of his blocking, and the answer would be "Moose" Johnston.

Johnston was a great blocking back, who would go on to have a career in which he ended up with more receptions than carries. His best season was 1993, when he caught fifty passes and averaged 7.4 yards a reception. He would end his career with twenty-two touchdown catches. Although Moose never ran the ball much, he is secure in the knowledge that he made key blocks hundreds of times for a running back, Smith, who would go on to become the league's all-time leading rusher.

Moose didn't get the limelight or the accolades that "the Triplets" (Aikman, Smith, and Irvin) did, but his peers and coaches knew full well the value Johnston brought to the locker room, the huddle, and the line of scrimmage. He has always been someone you could count on and is easy to deal with. No agendas with Daryl—just honest, upfront conversation.

The media also respected Johnston as much as they did any Cowboy of that era because, win or lose, he always made himself available for postgame comments. When the locker room got as quiet as a ghost town following a tough loss, most of the media knew our ace in the hole was No. 48. It was like an unwritten rule that the Moose would always be there to provide a sound bite when everyone else was clamming up, hustling off to the shower, or hiding in the trainer's room so they didn't have to talk.

I also had the opportunity to cohost *The Daryl Johnston Show.* Like Troy, when on the air, Johnston was a natural. And today, just like Troy, Moose is one of the top NFL analysts on network TV—likewise, on FOX.

Through it all, the one thing I have admired most about Johnston is his balance. He's well grounded. When Norwegian Cruise Lines asked me in 1994 to put together a cruise with some celebrities, I said I would do it if it benefited a charity. We chose Big Brothers Big Sisters, the nationally known mentoring nonprofit I had become involved with through my *Scott's Kids* weekly television program. So, the cruise became an event with the Cowboys—"The Super Bowl Champs Cruise the Caribbean."

The first player chosen, as my daughter would say, was a "no brainer." I picked Johnston because he's likeable, flexible, and a fan favorite. And, true to form, he connected with everybody on board, allowing everybody to connect with him.

Johnston enjoys giving back as well, getting involved with worthwhile charity events. In 1993, he teamed up with me to create "the Muscle Team" for the Muscular Dystrophy Association. Many players will lend their name and then disappear, never sticking around for the long haul. Not D.J. He has been involved with MDA ever since and has made some meaningful and lasting relationships with the boys and girls who have muscular dystrophy, not to mention the awareness and money he has helped us raise. The Muscle Team is now in sixteen cities across America and annually raises millions.

Daryl's wife, Diane, has also been an important part of the Muscle Team, having served as the event chairperson on several occasions. Notwithstanding her busy schedule, she's always anxious to help out, despite being a model by profession, a volunteer by choice, and a wife and mom out of love. She's adorable, and she's a dynamo. Whether she's raising money for kids or securing auction items for a cause, you just can't say no to Diane. I'll not soon forget the time she called me in a panic, looking for assistance in putting together a *This Is Your Life*-type video for D.J., who was about to celebrate his fortieth birthday. I immediately called my son, and next thing you know, Doug has everyone at our production company, Murray Media, creating, dubbing, picking out music, and going through scrapbooks and photo albums that dated back to Daryl's early days growing up in upstate New York. In the process, we got a number of his former teammates, friends, and family on camera, until it was completed. As it turned out, Johnston was thrilled when Diane gave it to him, and the minimovie debut at the party provided plenty of laughs, an abundance of emotion, and loads of fond memories for all in attendance. Mission accomplished.

Then there's Emmitt, the final piece of the Cowboys puzzle who came on board after a tremendous career at the University of Florida. Sixteen teams passed on him before the Cowboys got him with the No. 17 pick in the first round of the 1990 NFL draft. It was a steal, although it still took the Cowboys a while to get him signed.

Relatively small and not that fast, Emmitt quickly proved himself as someone who would not be denied. Don't tell Smith what he can or cannot do, because he will do everything in his power—and beyond at times, I'm convinced—to prove you wrong.

Coming out of Florida, Smith, at five feet nine and 199 pounds, was deemed too small and too slow by many scouts. These comments were similar to the knocks made by critics of Walter Payton when he was coming out of Jackson State in the mid-1970s. Too small? Too slow? Smith would skip, dart, and stutter-step his way to 18,355 career yards, along the way breaking Payton's all-time mark of 16,726 that had lasted more than fifteen years.

As a youngster, Emmitt had idolized Payton, often watching film of "Sweetness." The two would become friends in the 1990s, and Emmitt has remained close to the Payton family since Walter's death in 1999.

I'll never forget the final game of the 1993 season playing the Giants at the Meadowlands, when Emmitt played the second half and overtime with a separated shoulder, as the Cowboys really needed him in the backfield. Here was the scenario leading up to that: With Smith holding out that year, the Cowboys had started 0–2 before he finally signed and helped lead the Cowboys to victories in eleven of their next thirteen games. However, they still needed to beat the Giants in that final regular season game to secure homefield advantage and a first-round bye in the play-offs. Smith would finish with 229 total yards, 168 of them rushing, as he inspired the Cowboys to a 16–13 overtime victory over the Giants.

Smith finished that 1993 season with his third consecutive league rushing title, and he would cap it all off with a Super Bowl MVP performance as his two second-half touchdowns spurred the Cowboys to a 30–13 victory over the Buffalo Bills.

Smith played like a man possessed (not to mention a man in pain) in that victory over the Giants, and that was a defining moment in his Canton-esque career. Emmitt was the epitome of someone who would suck it up and play, when most others would simply pack it in and quit.

Smith was the ultimate team player, and like some of the other Cowboys, he, too, viewed giving back to the community to be as automatic as getting up in the morning. He's made a difference in many people's lives through his foundation, which he runs with his wife, Pat. She's a former television personality from California who sparkles with class, giving new meaning to the phrase "woman behind the man."

Aside from all the public appearances that seem never ending, Emmitt is now a part of another great team, working at the Staubach Company. He's taking that never-give-up attitude and applying it to the business world.

Roger just raves about the job that Emmitt is doing for him, saying he's most impressed with the intensity of Emmitt's desire to learn everything he can about the commercial real estate business. "Many guys at Emmitt's level normally don't do that," Roger told me, "instead, being content to try and live on their celebrity status."

It really was enjoyable covering those Cowboys in the early 1990s. There were a number of individuals with distinct personalities, but it all came down to getting it done as a team, collectively coming together as one.

That first year at the Super Bowl for this group (after the 1992 season) was especially fun, in large part because we found ourselves poolside for our five daily newscasts. How can you beat that? I was broadcasting from just in front of Santa Monica's famed pier for more than three hours a day. Rough assignment.

I love telling the story of my wife, Carole, flying out to California on the Wednesday morning of Super Bowl week. In getting ready for the trip the night before, she missed the 10:00 p.m. news segment in which I had legendary actor Gene Hackman on live as a guest, and he was terrific. Very entertaining. The next morning, after I picked up Carole at the airport, I was driving back to the hotel on Ocean Boulevard, and, wouldn't you know it, just as we were pulling up to valet parking, here comes Hackman walking out of the hotel.

Carole sees him and gets really excited, proclaiming, "Hey, look, it's Gene Hackman! I love him." As we hop out, I yell to him, "Good morning, Gene. What's up?" He looks up and, obviously remembering me from the show the night before, says, "Hey, Scott. How ya' doin'?"

I thought Carole was going to drop. She whispers over to me, "How does he know you?" At that point, he came over and met Carole, and he couldn't have been nicer.

The week was packed with interviews of TV and movie stars. Hopefully the whole experience was unforgettable for our viewers, because it sure was unforgettable for all of us. It was just a fun week. We wrapped it up with Jay Leno, who joined me to cohost *Scott Murray's Sports Extra* for more than two and a half hours, live from poolside, as the players arrived back at the hotel after the game. He was classic Leno, and I felt sort of like Ed McMahon as straight man for Johnny Carson, in my case setting up Leno for his one-liners. He was a good sport about the whole thing, obviously enjoying himself. In fact, he had Troy on the *Tonight Show* the very next night.

Cowboys owners Jerry and Gene Jones were kind enough to give us their first post–Super Bowl interview following the 52–17 victory over the Buffalo Bills. In the midst of it all, they started off laughing and saying how this moment seemed like déjà vu for them, recalling that I had been the first person to do a one-on-one interview with them just days after they had bought the Cowboys and come to Dallas in 1989. They were both so nervous before that initial interview, having little experience with the media. I must have spent ten minutes assuring and reassuring them the world wasn't about to come to an end. Jerry was also very emotional, even breaking down when he spoke about particular members of his family who had played a special role in his life. But now, four years later, the Super Bowl win brought nothing but smiles.

Despite how outspoken and controversial Jerry has been at times since buying the Cowboys in 1989, there is no debating his great business sense and deal-making ability. Whether it's signing a free agent, developing real estate tracts, or having the vision for any number of other ventures, Jones is usually on target. No wonder he's as proud of his Entrepenuer of the Year Award as he is of his three Lombardi Super Bowl Trophies. And one can only imagine what he has up his sleeve for the new stadium complex in Arlington that will soon house his Cowboys and other major events. The Jones family has always been accommodating and kind to me, publicly thanking me in April 2003 when I retired from television news. The entire family gathered at midfield at the American Airlines Center to honor me during the halftime of a play-off game of the Dallas Desperados, Jerry's Arena Football League Team. They presented me with a pair of signed football helmets, one from the Desperados and one from the Cowboys. The ceremony certainly wasn't necessary, but it was something I'll always cherish. Just as I'll cherish a similar gesture days earlier from the Dallas Stars between periods of their NHL regular season finale, when I received a personalized Stars hockey jersey from team president Jim Lites and the Stars organization. Such recognition is always appreciated, but it also reminds you that it's really a celebration of the outstanding television teams of which you have been a part. Without the opportunities I have been afforded and the teammates I've worked alongside, such recognition would likely never have come. So, for that, I'm eternally grateful.

Everybody has an opinion about America's Team, love 'em or hate 'em. At no time has that ever been more pronounced than during Super Bowl week, regardless of the year. Covering Super Bowl celebrations with the Cowboys involved is the ultimate kick. You don't sleep for a week, putting together thirty-minute specials, one after another, in addition to your three nightly sportscasts. But that's why you get into this business in the first place. As the station PR department always said in promoting the coverage, "It's live; it's local; it's late breaking." And for us, it seemed never ending. But it was great fun and quite rewarding in the end.

Those Cowboys of Jerry Jones, Jimmy Johnson, Troy Aikman, Emmitt Smith, Michael Irvin, Moose Johnston, et al., epitomized "team," just as those Cowboys teams of Tex Schramm, Gil Brandt, Tom Landry, Roger Staubach, Tony Dorsett, Drew Pearson, et al., did before them. It's what makes them competitive. It's what makes them successful. It's what makes them winners. And that's what it's all about—getting it done together as a team, winning as a group, being the best as a family, whatever it takes.

Family has always been first and foremost in my life. My parents instilled that culture within me and my two sisters at an early age. And later in life as a dad, I tried to instill that same culture in my own family. As I look back, there are definitely things I should have done differently, certainly times I could have made wiser choices. But through it all, I have few regrets. I've been most fortunate, occasionally lucky, and extremely blessed. As a result, I will be forever grateful for the opportunities I have been afforded, the lessons I have learned, and the friendships I have shared. And although I can't even begin to comprehend what Lou Gehrig must have had to endure when he learned his young life was about to be abruptly cut short by a disease that remains a death sentence to this day, it is a little easier for me to now understand why he considered himself to be "the luckiest man on the face of the earth."

Thanks, Dad!!

RESOURCES

aeispeakers.com

allamericanspeakers.com

answers.com

aol.nba.com

daveyobrien.com

Detroit Free Press

espn.com

espn.go.com

hickoksports.com

historicbaseball.com

leadingauthorities.com

motorsportshalloffame.com

nadiacomaneci.com

NFL Players Association

patsummerall.ambassadoragency.com

Philanthropy World magazine, March-April 2003

Pro Football Hall of Fame

Starpulse.com

Startribune.com

biography.com

tigerwoods.com

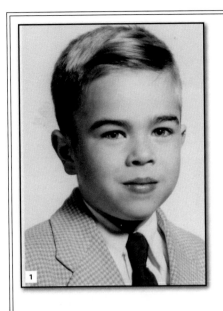

1. My second grade class picture (1957).

2. *GQ*, circa 1960.

3. Me with my proud dad and his ever-present pipe (1952).

1. Doug, Stephanie, and me, prior to my being named Father of the Year (2002).

2. My pride and joy . . . Stephanie and Doug (1984).

3. Mom and Dad (early '80s).

4. Doug, Stephanie, Carole, and me at an NFL pre-season game in San Diego (1988).

1. Teammates for life—Doug as our five-year-old batboy on TV station charity team (1979).

2. Doug and Coach Landry at Cowboys training camp in Thousand Oaks, California (1982).

3. Doug at legendary UCLA basketball coach John Wooden's summer camp in Thousand Oaks (1983).

4. Stephanie and 1982 Heisman Trophy winner Herschel Walker (1988).

5. Stephanie with NHL All-Star and Dallas Stars center Mike Modano (1995).

1. Broadcasting Cowboys pre-season game with Cowboys great and current Cowboys radio analyst Charlie Waters (1983).

2. Me, capturing a Kodak moment of my son Doug and Mickey Mantle (1985).
(Photo by David Woo—*The Dallas Morning News*.)

3. *Scott's Kids* Television Show on NBC Dallas–Fort Worth (1994).

1. Scott anchoring nightly sportscast on NBC Dallas–Fort Worth (1995).

2. NBC 5 News team at Super Bowl XXVII in Pasadena: Mike Snyder, Jane McGarry, and me (1993).

3. Interviewing Cowboys owners Gene and Jerry Jones following their first Super Bowl win at the Rose Bowl (1993).

4. Interviewing Cal Ripken Jr. before a live taping of TV show (2005).

5. Cohosting The Daryl Johnston Show (1997).

1. Mickey Mantle and me in the Texas Rangers dugout at the opening of the Ballpark in Arlington, now Ameriquest Field (1994).

2. A proud day for me, as I took part in carrying the flame in the Olympic Torch Run (1996).

3. Interviewing Jerry Jones at RFK Stadium in Washington DC immediately following his first win as the Cowboys owner (1989).

4. Daryl Johnston and me at his home, taking a break from taping an MDA spot (2006).

1. Getting ready to interview 49ers quarterback Steve Young, shortly after he was named MVP of Super Bowl XXIX in Miami (1995).

2. Interviewing UT football coach Mack Brown for a live broadcast to Texas from the Heisman Trophy ceremony at the Downtown Athletic Club in New York City (1998).

3. Interviewing Dallas Cowboys Cheerleaders at Super Bowl XXVII (1993).

1. Joining NASCAR's "first family" of the track, seven-time champion King Richard Petty and current Nextel Cup owner/driver Kyle Petty (2005).

2. Three-time Indy 500 champion Johnny Rutherford and me, prior to the Indianapolis 500 (1994).

3. Bowling in the Sam Hornish Jr. Celebrity Tournament benefiting the Speedway Children's Charity. Hornish is a three-time IRL champion and the 2006 Indy 500 winner (2006).

4. Me behind the wheel of a Formula Ford at the Bob Bondurant School of Racing in Phoenix (1996).

5. Me with fellow celebrity drivers, actor Parker Stephenson and singer/songwriter Christopher Cross, at Grand Prix of Dallas Formula One Race (1984).

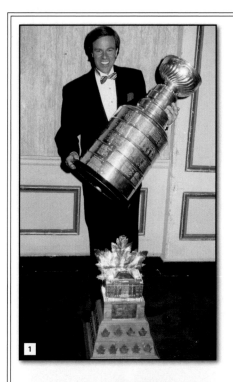

1. Me, holding the holy grail of hockey, Lord Stanley's Cup, after the Dallas Stars captured their first ever NHL title. I'm standing in front of the Conn Smythe Trophy, which is given to the MVP of the finals (1999).

2. Standing next to the "Great One," Wayne Gretzky (2000).

3. Dad and me alongside the Stanley Cup at the Hockey Hall of Fame in Toronto (1997).

1. SMU's famed "Pony Express" Eric Dickerson and Craig James, helping me auction sports memorabilia at the Doak Walker National Running Back Awards presentation banquet (2001).

2. Introducing the Doak Walker Awards keynote speaker, NFL Hall of Famer Walter Payton (1994).

3. Presenting Davey O'Brien National Quarterback Legends award winner Terry Bradshaw with a pair of western boots (2004).

1. 1981 Heisman Trophy winner and NFL Hall of Famer Marcus Allen (1998).

2. Former Cowboys wide receiver Drew "Hail Mary" Pearson (2005).

3. Being honored by FCA with my dad, my son, and my great friend, NFL Hall of Famer Bob Lilly (1996).

4. Emceeing the Night With a Champion event at the Fort Worth Club (1998).

5. NBA Hall of Famer Bill Russell of the Boston Celtics (2002).

6. Tennis Hall of Famer Chris Evert and sports commentator Mary Carillo (1998).

1. Presenting an award to sports visionary Lamar Hunt at the Dallas All-Sports Association awards banquet (2003).

2. Hoping that the talent representing seven Super Bowl wins might rub off on me as I stand next to Hall of Fame quarterbacks Terry Bradshaw (four titles) and Troy Aikman (three titles) in front of the Davey O'Brien National Quarterback trophy (2004).

3. Serving as master of ceremonies at the Cotton Bowl Classic luncheon (1998).

1. Texas Rangers owner Tom Hicks and me with the two greatest defensive catchers in the history of baseball. Johnny Bench (standing next to me) has ten Gold Glove Awards, while Ivan "Pudge" Rodriguez has eleven (2002).

2. Three generations of Murray's: Me with my dad and my son (2001).

3. A copy of a picture that hangs proudly in my study. I'm flanked by golf icons Byron Nelson and Ben Hogan at the Fort Worth Hall of Fame induction ceremony (1987).

1. Pro Football Hall of Famer and FOX football studio analyst Howie Long (1997).

2. NBC and HBO Emmy Award–winning sportscaster and host Bob Costas (1993).

3. Chris "Boomer" Berman, whom I've known since he joined ESPN in 1979 (1997).

4. CBS play-by-play sportscaster and host Greg Gumbel (1996).

1. Two-time Masters champion and golf good guy Ben Crenshaw (2001).

2. Three-time NCAA basketball champion and 2008 U.S. Olympic Team basketball coach Mike Krzyzewski (1997).

3. Former National League MVP and current ESPN broadcaster Joe Morgan (2004).

4. Basketball Hall of Famer and NBA executive Jerry West (2004).

5. Hitching a ride alongside "the Bus," Super Bowl XL winner and NBC football analyst Jerome Bettis (2006).

6. NY Yankees manager Joe Torre (2004).

1. Former heavyweight champion George Foreman, who taught me not only how to look tough but how to grill as well (2001).

2. Former welterweight champion Sugar Ray Leonard, whom I met at the 1976 Olympics in Montreal (2004).

3. Gale Sayers, youngest player ever voted into the Pro Football Hall of Fame (1991).

4. Pat Riley, second winningest coach in NBA history, with five league championships (1989).

5. Eight-time tennis Grand Slam winner Andre Agassi (1990).

6. Tennis Hall of Famer Jimmy Connors (1987).

1. Baseball Hall of Fame pitcher Nolan Ryan and Country Music Hall of Fame singer Charlie Pride (1991).

2. Seven-time Tour de France winner Lance Armstrong (2002).

3. Sports and golf icon Arnold Palmer (1993).

1. Washington Redskins Super Bowl coach and NASCAR team owner Joe Gibbs (1993).

2. Penn State football coach Joe Paterno, who has more wins than any other major college coach in history (1992).

3. President George Bush, former general managing partner of the Texas Rangers, at the governor's mansion in Austin, Texas (1997).

4. The tall and the short of it: Me with Hall of Famer Kareem Abdul-Jabbar (1994).

5. I also came up short next to "the Doctor," Hall of Famer Julius Erving (1989).

1. Like father, like son. Former Dallas Cowboys running back and 2005 Father of the Year Calvin Hill and his son, NBA All-Star Grant, along with me (2002 Father of the Year) and my son, Doug (2004).

2. In the middle of another father-son combo with lots of quarterbacking talent. Two-time NFL Most Valuable Player Peyton Manning and his dad, former all-pro Archie (2004).

3. Basketball Hall of Famers Isiah Thomas and Magic Johnson, two members of my all-star team for the Spud Webb celebrity game benefiting the Boys and Girls Club of Dallas (1988).

1. On the ice at the 2000 NHL All-Star Game at the Air Canada Center in Toronto with my dad (on my right) and his brother, my uncle Howie.

2. I'm bookended by two of the best sportscasters of all-time, Dick Enberg and Pat Summerall (2005).

3. Two of the greatest athletes in the history of SMU, "Dandy" Don Meredith and the legendary "Doaker," Doak Walker (1995).

4. All five of the Heisman Trophy winners from the service academies (clockwise from me):
Pete Dawkins, Army (1958); Roger Staubach, Navy (1963); Joe Bellino, Navy (1960); Felix "Doc" Blanchard, Army (1945); and Glenn Davis, Army (1946).

SCOTT MURRAY

1. With Jay Leno, who, in 1993, cohosted *Scott Murray's Sports Extra* following Super Bowl XXVII (1999).

2. Preparing for a Special Olympics clinic with gold medalists Nadia Comeniche and Bart Conner (1996).

3. Two Texas golfing greats, Lee Trevino and Lanny Wadkins (2004).

4. Receiving an award from Big Brothers Big Sisters of America honorary national chairman and Baseball Hall of Famer Hank Aaron (1991).

5. On the ice with Olympic gold medalist Dorothy Hamill (1996).

1. Tom Landry, third-winningest NFL coach of all time, and Don Shula, winningest NFL coach of all-time (1995).

2. Saying hello to Pat and Emmitt Smith, the NFL all-time career leader in rushing yards (2001).

3. My son, Doug, and his all-time favorite athlete, Hall of Fame quarterback John Elway (2000).

1. Surrounded by four of the greatest running backs in the history of football (left to right): Earl Campbell, Tony Dorsett, Walter Payton, and Emmitt Smith (1993).

2. Tony Dorsett, on hand to flip the coin at the inaugural PlainsCapital Fort Worth Bowl (2003).

3. Former NFL commissioner Paul Tagliabue (2005).

4. Roger Staubach and Troy Aikman about to appear live on *Scott Murray's Sports Extra* at the Cowboys' inaugural training camp at St. Edward's University in Austin (1990).

1. In my study at home, surrounded by plenty of great memories (2002).

2. My college DJ days, spinning records at a club called the Varsity Inn (1971).

3. Dad and I, prior to my driving in the Grand Prix of Dallas (1994).

4. My mentor and friend, my dad, for whom this book was written (2006).